The **POWER** *in*
His Presence

Tap into God's Presence and receive Power
to fulfil your divine assignment.

TORI TANEKA

I have known Tori for 4 years as a faithful member of our Church. She is a woman of worship and of the word of God, seeking to know Him more, and glorify Him, in how she lives and also through her appearance, knowing that she is a Temple of the living God. She is gentle, but strong in the Lord. I have seen her in difficult situations, BUT not one critical word, complaint or 'upset' ever came from her. I vividly remember how she dealt with a particularly frustrating circumstance that would have stressed even the most placid of temperaments, but not once in the 'fiasco' that took place did she show anything negative. She was her usual calm and lovely person. She is a woman of integrity who lives her Christian faith every day. I know that I can always depend on Victoria, whatever the circumstances. I highly recommend her book to you, which she has written from her heart with diligence and accuracy, the fruit of her spiritual journey in the Lord.

—*Hilary Walker, Assistant Pastor, Oxford Bible Church, UK.*

It's practical! It's powerful! The knowledge and revelation in this book will undoubtedly draw you closer to God. A guide on how we should live as Temples of God in His Presence. This is pure gold mined from the scriptures for a richer, more meaningful relationship with God.

I highly recommend "The Power in His Presence" for anybody that hungers and thirsts for His Presence.

—*Sandra Taneka, Harare, Zimbabwe.*

I have recently read the book 'The Power in His Presence'. It is a book that reveals in detail how the Temple of God works, how it can work with you and the parallels it has to Jesus. This book goes really in depth about the Temple but breaks it down into easy sections.

A piece that really enlightened me was about the Menorah, the Golden Lampstand; how this relates to Jesus as the light of the world. On a day I was faced with a seemingly difficult task concerning my mum's care, I read about this piece as I waited in the nurse's office. Applying what I read to my situation made it seem easier and enlightened my mood, it really changed things for the better.

I have been a Christian for 30 years and found this book an easy read. "The Power in His Presence", will help you on your spiritual journey to get that closeness to God. The prayer at the end of each section is valuable and practical for our everyday lives.

—*Camilla Comley, Oxford, UK.*

DEDICATIONS

To my beloved mum Christine, who from her womb brought me forth into this world. Mum, for all your toil over the years, your intercession, yours counsel, 1 am forever grateful. I am today because of you.

To my beloved sister Sandra, thank you for standing by me through thick and thin. Thank you for your counsel, your prayers and all the laughter we share every season of the soul. What a treasure you are and 1 love doing life with you.

Chiefly, to the King of Kings, the Lord of my life, 1 am highly indebted to You Abba Father. For loving me with an everlasting love, for great grace, and for Your Presence 1 am forever grateful to you Lord. And 1 confess Heavenly Father that you are the real deal. Nothing in this world will ever satisfy me, but Your Presence. There is nothing quite like your Presence Lord!

ACKNOWLEDGEMENTS

To all the men and women of God who has poured into my life over the years, to all the sisters and brothers in the Lord l have had the opportunity to fellowship with, and to my family, l appreciate you deeply.

May the good Lord richly bless you.

FOREWORD

by Derek Walker, Pastor of Oxford Bible Church

It is my great pleasure to commend this informative and inspiring book: 'The Power in His Presence' by Tori Taneka. The Lord Jesus said: "The hour is coming, and now is, when the true worshipers will worship the Father in spirit and truth; for the Father is seeking such to worship Him. God is Spirit, and those who worship Him must worship in spirit and truth" (John 4:23-24). As Tori's Pastor, I can assure you that she is a true worshipper, who seeks to know her God more and more, and abide in His Presence. She is also a diligent student of His Word, knowing that His Word is Truth (John 17:17), our authoritative and trustworthy guide into the spiritual realities that are ours in Christ. She has come to realise that all the life, power, wisdom, victory and blessings of God are freely given to us, but they are located in His Presence - in Christ Himself, so it is only as we learn to draw close to Him and enter into His Presence, that we can draw upon His Power, and so glorify Him in our lives.

God has made us to be Temples of His Holy Spirit, reflecting and shining His glory. When man lost the Presence and Glory of God through sin, He made a Way back into His Presence for us through Christ and laid down a blueprint for us in His Word for how we can enter into His Presence and receive His Power for living. Much of this revelation is encoded in the Tabernacle of Moses, based on the instructions God gave him on Mount Sinai. Using the blueprint of the Tabernacle, Tori leads us on an exciting journey from the Outer Court into the Holy of Holies, where we can enjoy intimate fellowship with God in His Presence, and be filled with His Power. She shares many deep and precious insights that she has discovered in God's Word that will enrich your spiritual life and help you in your own personal journey into the fullness of God's Presence.

In Christ (in His Presence) all the fullness of God dwells (Colossians 1:19); in Christ are hidden all the treasures of wisdom and knowledge (Colossians 2:3); we have been blessed with every spiritual blessing of God in Christ (Ephesians 1:3); our life and destiny is hidden with Christ in God (Colossians 3:3); and in His Presence is fullness of joy (Psalm 16:11). What's more, He is our life (Colossians 3:4), and Christ, our life, is in us, the hope of glory! (Colossians 1:27). So all of these realities have been freely given to us and made available to us in Christ, having been purchased by His precious Blood, and Christ is in us, in the holy of holies of our spirit. He has broken down every barrier separating us from Him, signified by the torn veil of the Temple. He has prepared the Way, and now He invites us to press into His Presence by faith and possess

His grace and power for our lives. Therefore, it should be our highest priority to abide in Christ, and partake of His life, love and Power. It is important to understand that all things will forever belong to Christ and exist in Christ, but because He ever gives Himself to us, we can continually enjoy and experience His abundant life. The more we enter into His Presence, the more His Presence will flow out from our spirits and enter into and fill our hearts, empowering our souls and our lives.

After teaching us about how to enter into God's Presence and receive the grace and power that comes from His Presence, Tori then teaches us about how we can then activate and release God's grace and power in our lives for His glory. It is one thing to receive His power, it is another thing to live, walk and operate in the Power of His Spirit. As Temples of the Living God, it is not enough for us to possess His Spirit within us, but to allow His Spirit to flow through us in our lives. The life of Christ within us is meant to be expressed and manifested in our outer lives. She shares how we can pull down the strongholds of fear and doubt, which paralyse us, and she teaches us how we can build our God-confidence to act on His Word and shine His light, knowing who we are in Christ, and who Christ is in us. Faith without corresponding actions is dead (inoperative, unfruitful and ineffective), so our obedient actions of faith are necessary for God's glory to be manifested through us. The natural working together with the supernatural Power of God produces the fruit that God desires from us.

I highly recommend this book to you, which will feed your faith and call you into a higher life in the Lord, so that you will be able to increasingly tap into the Power of His Presence to fulfil your Divine Assignment, and to shine forth His glory through the outward order, harmony and beauty of your life, to the glory of God.

CONTENTS

INTRODUCTION

*"That I may know Him and the Power of His
resurrection" (Philippians 3:10)*

S uddenly I found myself sitting in this peculiar room with a rectangular shape which was possibly thirty feet long and ten feet wide. The room had a slight aura of dimness and an ancient feel to it, and its walls were of rubble-stone masonry. It had two doors, one for coming in at the bottom right side of the room and an exit in the wall toward the front left side of the room. Within the room were eight rows of chairs, with about five chairs in a row. On my left side was my sister in the Lord; behind us were twenty to thirty strangers who all seemed to know each other. There was a large screen right ahead of us on the wall, so I perceived we were in some cinema room. As I sat there patiently, I wondered why we were waiting. However, asking anyone under the prevailing circumstances was absurd, so I continued playing the waiting game. Then, suddenly, a light projected on to the wall ahead; lo and behold, the movie had begun!

I

I recalled that one night about 16 weeks before then, while at home in Oxford, I lay on my bed at around one o'clock in the morning trying hard to get some sleep, but I could not sleep a wink. I was not troubled in mind or spirit; if anything, I had the Lord's peace. I did not feel like doing anything that required a lot of attention either, such as reading. Eventually, I realised the Lord was trying to get my attention though I could not immediately discern what He wanted me to do. As I lay on the bed in anticipation with my face looking up at the ceiling, I suddenly remembered that in 16 weeks' time, I would be travelling to Israel. I was going along with my sister in the Lord to attend a 3-day women's conference north of Israel in Magdala. We were going there for six days and did not have plans regarding the rest of the trip to South Israel, Jerusalem.

Earlier in the year 2019, we had been to Israel for a pilgrimage tour with my church. It was a large group, just large enough to fill up a 52-seater coach. On one of our days during this pilgrimage tour, we visited a place called Magdala Worship Centre. As the tour guide showed us around, she mentioned a women's conference called "Encounter", which was coming up the following year in March. As soon as I heard about the conference, my heart skipped with excitement. I felt a prompting to enquire about this conference shortly after the guided tour, and I approached the guide to make further inquiries. This exceedingly kind and warm lady with an Irish accent filled me in regarding the conference and gave me some flyers with details. I was not crystal clear then about conference details, however, on the other hand, my heart was captivated by the story of Mary of Magdala.

Mary was a woman possessed with seven demons before meeting Jesus. When Mary encountered Jesus, the trajectory of her life changed for good. She was completely delivered and decided to go hard after Jesus. She served the Lord with her all and even followed Him right to the foot of the cross. In my spirit, I knew right away I had to come back for this conference which would take place the first quarter of the following year. As we headed back to the coach, I mentioned this to the lady I sat next to. I did not know her then; we just found ourselves sitting next to each other on the coach we were using for our tour and became regular coach buddies. We both shared a mutual feeling about the conference and the Worship Centre, and we agreed to come back the following year for this event.

Shortly after our return from our pilgrimage tour, we reserved our hotels for our 2020 trip back to Israel and then paid for our flights a couple of weeks later. We planned to stay a bit longer than the three-day conference to do some more exploring; therefore, we needed to make plans for the rest of our trip to Israel. So, during the year, I began praying to the Lord for divine direction.

As I continued to lie on the bed that night, my thoughts suddenly flew to our upcoming Israel trip, and I was full of excitement yet again. In the spur of the moment, I reached out for my laptop and started browsing on the internet to find places of interest we could go to for the remainder of the week during our time there. Suddenly, memories of my previous tour awakened; I got so engrossed with all the places we could visit and the things we could do. Come 4:30 am I was still up, and thankfully I had taken time off work that week. To my surprise, I planned and even wrote an itinerary for the rest of our trip that night.

I designed it to the last detail: from our departure in the UK to every day we spent in Israel, the time and duration at every site we would visit, our commute details, and I made online reservations for all the places I could on that night. I even planned our car parking here in the UK at the airport. At that point, I was ready and raring to go. The power of the internet! I feel so blessed to be born in such a time like this. I suddenly felt a release to sleep, and I knew then that I had accomplished my intended mission.

Fast forward to March 2020 while in Jerusalem, as I sat in this movie room with my eyes now glued on the screen, I was thinking to myself, this was not my plan to be here. I felt cheated. Before our trip to Israel, I asked the Lord to speak to me and give me a clear word and revelation during this trip. As I was pondering and reflecting on our journey so far, one thing stood out for me, and it was "The Temple of God". In pretty much all the places we had seen, even at the conference, I could see a common thread connecting all these places and highlighting "The Temple of God". I knew then that the Lord was speaking to me specifically about "His Holy Temple". It was so silently loud in my heart, my mind, and my spirit.

So, on our last day in Jerusalem, we spent some time in the morning in the garden tomb, the site of burial and resurrection of our Lord Jesus. We meditated, broke bread together, and lingered in the sweetness of His Presence. We gave ourselves just enough time, 30 minutes to be precise, to get to the Davidson Centre Archaeological Park for our pre-booked guided tour of the park, which was our final tour for the day and the trip itself.

Unfortunately, we got lost a couple of times along the way, and consequently, we were about seven minutes late for the tour. At that point, we had missed our designated tour guide and group, so I headed to reception to ask if they could do anything for us. The kind lady at the reception gladly offered us the option to go on the next similar tour, which was three hours long and lasted from 2 pm till 5 pm. However, this slot was not convenient as we were flying back home to the

UK on that day and were supposed to be at Tel-Aviv airport at 5 pm for our check-in. The next best thing she had was an hour-long unguided access to the museum at the Davidson Centre, which was literally across the road. I thought something was better than nothing, and we accepted the offer. However, within me, I felt somewhat disappointed that we missed a good three-hour tour that promised to be quite exciting and had to settle for an hour of unguided visit.

I had planned this about four months ago, I thought to myself, and was even paid up, only to find out at the eleventh hour that we cannot make it! At that point, I felt a loss of my joy as we sadly walked across to the other side of the road to tour the museum, to which we were granted an hour's worth of access. As we went in, there was a tour group right ahead of us with a guide. So cheekily, we decided to follow them and listen to what their tour guide was teaching them. As we walked down the corridor of the museum, the group walked through two small rooms with some fascinating archaeological displays, and we were there right behind them. Eventually, they arrived at this room where they all began to sit down and fill up the chairs starting from the backbenches and leaving the front row empty.

As we were at the back of the crowd, we did not have many options left as to where to sit, so we walked right up to the front row, sat there, and with straight faces, looked to the front where pretty much everybody was facing. I certainly think the rest of the group were now wondering who these two strangers they seem to have picked up along the way were, but no one dared to ask. So, we stayed with them as they did not seem too troubled about our presence.

And suddenly, the front wall was lit up, and on the screen appeared this young, tall, and handsome-looking man. The movie had begun. It turned out this man was a pilgrim back in the olden times during the Second Temple era, who had travelled from afar so he could come to the Temple of God in Jerusalem to worship the Lord; my heart was immediately captivated. I suddenly forgot about my disappointment. l felt my joy rush back to me, and my eyes fixed on the film with such joy and excitement. We watched the pilgrim's journey from the time he arrived in Jerusalem, went to the Temple to have his money changed, and bought his sacrificial animal. He then went for the ritual cleansing before he could get into the Temple of God. This film was approximately 15 minutes long, and it ended right at the "Temple" in Jerusalem where this young man had headed to worship. He stood there, perhaps feeling euphoric and accomplished, as he stood looking right at the Temple of God.

At that point, I could not stop laughing hysterically, and I thought the Lord had such a wonderful sense of humour. I could see the funny side to it but I also felt ashamed of myself. After reflecting on my journey in Israel so far, I strongly sensed the Lord was speaking to me about His Holy Temple. The previous night I foolishly asked the Lord yet again to confirm what he was saying to me on this trip. I had walked into this museum feeling annoyed that I had missed the 3-hour tour I had arranged a few months back, but the Lord impressed this on my heart: "This is the very reason I had you come here". I did not miss the 3-hour tour by accident; the Lord Himself orchestrated this. He ordered my steps so that I could be in the right place at the right time and see what He wanted me to focus on in this season, without leaving room for any doubt: right where this film ended "His Holy Temple".

The Lord had confirmed yet again what He wanted me to see and perceive, "His Holy Temple". I immediately felt a release in my spirit. I could hear my heart echoing the exact words of the Lord on the cross "It is finished", my mission indeed in Israel was accomplished. We still had another 35 to 40 minutes' worth of access to the museum to explore, and as I turned my head to my sister in the Lord, she felt the same that we had indeed accomplished our mission in the Holy land, and it was time to go back home to the UK. So, we quietly parted ways with the group that we had attached ourselves to. We hung around for a few minutes at the Archaeological Park to take a couple of photos outside the museum, as it is customary for me to have selfies. We then went back to the hotel to pick up our luggage and headed straight to the airport.

As I sat on the plane about 36,0000 feet above the ground, I began thinking about why the Lord was directing my attention specifically to "His Holy Temple" in this season. Suddenly, it dawned on me that as I committed my year to the Lord in prayer and fasting, I had asked Him that I might know Him more. In my quest, I prayed Apostle Paul's prayer, *"That I may know Him and the Power of His resurrection"* (Philippians 3:10), the same power that raised our Lord Jesus Christ from the dead (Ephesians 1:19-21 CEV), and I began to see the dots connecting.

In the fullness of time, I put pen to paper. I began to write this book, "The Power in His Presence". As I wrote this book, I had in mind the child of God who is dissatisfied with just going to church every Sunday and singing lovely songs, a child of God who is wondering if there is more to being a child of God than this. Perhaps the Lord has called you into church ministry, entrepreneurship, or the corporate world. You might be feeling stuck where you are and can't see the way out, or maybe you might have just believed the lies and deceit of the enemy that you are not good enough, not pretty enough, and not worth much after all. Maybe your relationship with the Lord feels so dry and you are longing for a deep and more meaningful relationship with Him. Or perhaps you are at a place where you have seen explosive breakthroughs in your life in the past, you saw the hand of God moving on your behalf and lifting you, but you are now feeling discontent, stuck, or restless. There is perhaps a stirring in your spirit, and the Spirit of the Lord is prompting you and saying to you, "You have dwelt at this mountain for far too long; it is time for you to break forth".

You see, there is always a higher dimension you can go to in your walk with God. So, beloved, I invite you to come along with me on an exciting journey that leads into the very Presence of God; so that you may know Him intimately and know how to continually access and enjoy His Presence. In His Presence, we receive vision, revelation, wisdom, and divine empowerment so that we can soar with wings like an eagle. I present this book to you to inspire and empower you so that you can tap into the Power that comes from the Presence of God and rise boldly to do what God is calling you to do, in His name and for His glory.

Beloved, I pray that as you read this book, you will open your heart, mind, and spirit and allow the Spirit of God to minister to you in fresh ways. I pray that you will receive revelation from on high, as well as experience transformation. May you be inspired and empowered to rise to your calling. May these words echo in your heart and be your unwavering and bold confession henceforth that "My Body is a Temple of the Living God" (1 Corinthians 6:19), a Temple full of the Power of God. You are indeed a masterpiece and a powerhouse, a carrier of the treasure of His Holy Spirit, created to bring glory and honour to His name.

Shalom!

Introduction

SECTION A

HIS PRESENCE

CAST OUT

From the beginning of time, God intended to dwell in the midst of His people, to have continual fellowship with them, and to make them His Temple. He intended to fill us with His Presence so that we would be carriers of His Presence and glory and that through us, His Spirit would flow out into the world as rivers of living water. The Temple notion goes back to the beginning of creation in the book of Genesis, right in the Garden of Eden, when the Temple concept was first introduced to man. God planted a garden on the east side of Eden, commonly known as the Garden of Eden.

*"The Lord God planted a garden eastward in Eden;
and there He put the man whom He had formed. And
out of the ground the Lord God made every tree grow
that is pleasant to the sight, and good for food. The tree
of life was also in the midst of the garden, and the tree
of knowledge of good and evil"* (Genesis: 2:8-9).

God created earth to be the dwelling place for man. The Garden of Eden was where God Himself would come down to walk and talk with Adam and Eve. Scripture tells us about God walking in the cool of the day in the garden seeking to speak with Adam and Eve (Genesis 3:8-9). It was a special place where God would relate to the people He created, a place where Adam and Eve could enjoy a relationship with the Lord and live a blessed life, filled and surrounded by His Presence. On the west side of Eden was a mountain from which a river of water flowed into the Garden of Eden to water it. The Garden of Eden was on a higher ground than the rest of Eden, and from the Garden of Eden, this river would part into four river heads as it cascaded to water the rest of the earth (Genesis 2:10-14). Eden was the source of all water on the earth.

If we look at this in parallel to the Temple of God, we see some similarities. Water coming from a higher place represents the Spirit of God. The mountain is the higher place where the water, representing the Spirit of God, flowed from into the Garden of Eden. The garden itself represents our soul, which we are responsible for cultivating and guarding, and which receives from the Spirit of God as we surrender to Him. When God created man, he gave him dominion over the earth and told him to be fruitful and multiply (Genesis 1:28). As we surrender to God, allow the river of God to flow into our hearts, so that as we tend to our souls, we become fruitful. The more our soul is submitted, the more infilling of His Spirit we receive. The water flowing out from the Garden of Eden is a picture of the Spirit of God in us flowing out to the world as rivers of living water, as we give of ourselves in service to humanity and in response to God's calling upon our lives.

The Lord God took the man and placed him in the Garden of Eden, to cultivate and guard it (Genesis 2:15). Interestingly the original Hebrew word for "Eden" translates to meanings such as: *"pleasure, fertility,* and refinement". It, therefore, makes sense to relate and understand the Garden of Eden in such terms as pleasurable or enjoyable and fruitful. Moreover, God placed Adam in the Garden of Eden for "guarding" (which is *"Shomrah"* in Hebrew), and for "cultivating," which translates from the Hebrew word *"Avodah"*. Avodah, the same Hebrew word used by priests in the Temple, is used in the context of the working of the soil. It makes sense then to conclude that the work that God commissioned man to do in the Garden of Eden was an act of service and worship unto God. Therefore, whatever God has called you to do, it is your act of service and worship unto Him, whether it is in business, full-time church ministry, in the corporate world, the community at large, or even in your family.

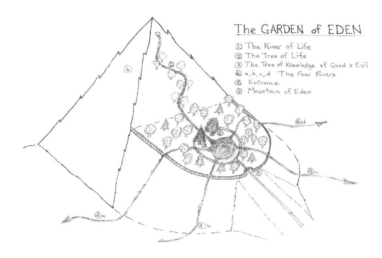

The GARDEN of EDEN
① The River of Life
② The Tree of Life
③ The Tree of Knowledge of Good & Evil
④ a, b, c, d   The Four Rivers
⑤ Entrance
⑥ Mountain of Eden

A Temple is a place where God would manifest His Presence, make Himself known to His people and speak with them. There are quite a few interesting features about the Garden of Eden that resemble the Temples of God, which man later constructed. These features make it apparent that the Garden of Eden was very much an archetype of the Temple of God. Below are some of these features:

- The Entrance to the Garden of Eden was on the east side of Eden. When God gave Moses instruction for the construction of the Tabernacle, he specified that the entrance would face the east. Solomon's Temple followed the same pattern.

- The Presence of God was made known in the Garden of Eden, and He would walk with His people in there. Likewise, the Tabernacle and the Temple were places where the Presence of God was, and He would make Himself known to His people and talk to them there.

◉ The Lord placed Adam in the garden to cultivate it and guard it. Likewise, the Levite Priests served God in the Tabernacle by protecting it from anything that defiles, and also had the responsibility of ministering in the Tabernacle or Temple.

◉ A river went out from Eden into the garden to water it, and then from the Garden of Eden, it parted into four rivers to water the rest of Eden and the earth. Likewise, in Ezekiel's vision of the Millennial Temple (Ezekiel 47:1-12), a river will flow out from the throne of God and we also see a river running from the throne of God in the Heavenly Temple (Revelation 22:1-3).

◉ The Mountain of God: God planted the Garden of Eden on a high place from which water would cascade down to water the rest of Eden. A mountain is a feature that was synonymous with the Temples. We also see this feature in the location of Solomon's Temple.

◉ The presence of the Cherubim: The cherubim were known to guard the way to the Presence of God. When man sinned, God placed the cherubim to guard the

Tree of Life (which was in the midst of the garden) from sinful man. So likewise, in the Holy of Holies inside the Tabernacle, were cherubim guarding the way to the Presence of God.

These points above are not exhaustive, but all highlight the common concepts between the Garden of Eden and the Temples of God. The Garden of Eden was indeed a Temple of God.

Sadly, Adam and Eve fell into sin. They did the very thing that the Lord asked them not to do. They ate of the fruit of knowledge of good and evil, which in turn, corrupted the rest of humanity as we are all their descendants. Because of their sin, Adam and Eve consequently lost the privilege to be in the Garden of Eden and to fellowship with Him. They were tragically cast out of the garden, further from God's Presence, because our God is holy. The Lord then placed the cherubim to the east of the garden to guard the Tree of Life from sinful man. Men could no longer approach God, except through blood sacrifices (Genesis 4:3-4). Outside the garden on the eastern side was a place of sacrifice, a picture and pattern we will see in the later Temples.

When the Lord had planted the garden east of Eden and placed Adam in there, *"And the Lord God commanded the man, saying, 'Of every tree of the garden you may freely eat; but of the tree of the knowledge of good and evil you shall not eat, for in the day that you eat of it you shall surely die'"* (Genesis 2:16-17). After Adam and Eve's disobedience and casting further from God's Presence, sin entered the world. The commission to work, which God once gave to Adam as a service to Him, we no longer associate with pleasure but with struggle and toil (Genesis 3:17). In the Garden of Eden was the Presence of God, and humanity could walk with God and have a relationship with Him, and in there was the privilege to worship God. In His Presence, there was fruitfulness, abundance, and there was life. Outside the garden, life was no longer the same without the same Presence of God.

Interestingly outside the garden, actual death began to happen as Cain murders Abel. Mankind now had to toil and sweat for them to eat. Because of this distance from the Presence of God, the wickedness of man continued to grow and multiply through generations, as witnessed in the days of Noah and in Sodom and Gomorrah when the Lord had to intervene in judgement and destroy His people, save a few righteous to preserve humanity.

This sinful state of man, separated from the Presence of God, was only temporary as God, who sees the end from the beginning, had long foreseen the fall of man and made a provision beforehand. Thus, our Lord Jesus was appointed to redeem us at a set time because of God's love for His people.

THE INVITATION

"And let them make Me a sanctuary, that I may dwell among them" (Exodus 25:8)

Meanwhile, the Lord took a temporary initiative to restore the broken relationship between Him and man because of God's love for you and I, so that He could be in the midst of His people again. He made a way for us to be able to come into His Presence, to fellowship, and to be able to hear from Him. God made a provision that was subject to protocol, that was to be followed by man. When he encountered Him at Mount Sinai, the Lord asked Moses to speak to the children of Israel and said, *"And let them make Me a sanctuary, that I may dwell among them. According to all that I show you,* that is, *the pattern of the Tabernacle and the pattern of all its furnishings, just so you shall make it"* (Exodus 25:8-9). The wilderness Tabernacle was God's temporary dwelling place and the Israelite's house of worship during their exodus from Egypt to the land of promise. This earthly and man-made Tabernacle was a copy of the true Tabernacle, the heavenly Temple. King Solomon eventually built the Jerusalem Temple to be the Israelite's permanent house of worship. Following its destruction, the second Temple superseded it. The Tabernacle reveals a pathway that we can also follow, leading us to God's Presence. In the protocol of entering the Tabernacle, its treasures, and materials, God showed a pattern for how His people could approach His Presence and have an intimate relationship with Him.

"Your way, O God, is in the sanctuary"
(Psalm 77:13)

The Lord specified, as He spoke to Moses, what materials were to be used to build this sanctuary, the Tabernacle. *"Then the Lord spoke to Moses, saying: Speak to the children of Israel, that they bring me an offering. From everyone who gives it willingly with his heart, you shall take my offering. And this is the offering which you shall take from them: gold, silver, and bronze; blue, purple, and scarlet thread, fine linen, and goats' hair; ram skins dyed red, badger skins, and acacia wood; oil for the light, and spices for the anointing oil and for the sweet incense;*

onyx stones, and stones to be set in the ephod and in the breastplate" (Exodus 25:1-7). The people provided materials in excess for the building of the Tabernacle and also gave their services freely. The materials used in constructing the Tabernacle and the choice of colours had meanings and significance, which can help us gain a richer understanding of the Tabernacle. Below are some clues in the context of the Tabernacle about some of the materials used.

- Gold – is a colour that signifies Deity.
- Silver – signifies Redemption.
- Bronze – represents Judgement.
- Blue – represents heavenliness or the Holy Spirit.
- Purple – is a colour that means Royalty or Kingship.
- Scarlet – symbolises the blood of Jesus.
- White or fine linen – signifies Purity.
- Goat's or Ram's hair – is for the covering and they signify atonement.
- Acacia wood – represents the humanity of Jesus and us also.
- Oil – is a picture of the Holy Spirit.

In this chapter, 1 will give you an overview of the Tabernacle, which 1 will further explore in the following chapters. As you read through the following chapters, you will journey through the biblical times of old, right back into the wilderness Temple. This is an exciting journey that leads us into the very Presence of God. We will see that every part of the Tabernacle had a purpose, meaning, and was rich with hidden treasures to unearth. *"It is the glory of God to conceal a matter, but the glory of kings to search out a matter"* (Proverbs 25:2).

"It is the glory of God to conceal a matter, but the glory of kings to search out a matter" (Proverbs 25:2).

As we move along this journey, I would also like you to bear in mind that today our bodies are the present and ultimate temples of God. However, from the richness of the Tabernacle structure, we can mine a wealth of knowledge to apply in our own lives that will help usher us into the Presence of God, where we can receive the Power that comes from His Presence. As we learn to abide in His Presence, we can continually enjoy and draw upon the life, grace, power, wisdom, victory over sin that flows from His Presence. We also receive revelational knowledge of His will concerning our lives.

The Tabernacle Overview

Interestingly, when the Lord gave Moses instruction at Mount Sinai for the Tabernacle's construction, He first gave instructions for the overview of the Ark of the Covenant and not the Tabernacle itself. I believe this was a message in itself emphasising the importance of the Ark of the Covenant. The reason and ultimate goal for entering the Tabernacle was to be where the Presence and glory of God was. The Ark of the Covenant was in the very last court of the Tabernacle, called the Holy of Holies, and above the Ark was a cover called the Mercy Seat. From above the Mercy Seat and between the two cherubim, the Lord would speak to His people. Though the children of Israel could walk freely through the Tabernacle gate into its Outer Court as they brought their sacrifice, there remained a need to get into the Holy of Holies; otherwise, all their efforts and sacrifices were in vain. Back then, only the High Priest would enter into the Holy of Holies on behalf of all the people of God.

Today the veil of separation that stood between the Holy Place and the Holy of Holies no longer stands, it was rent from top to bottom when Jesus was crucified. We no longer have to wait for the High Priest to enter in on our behalf. The ultimate goal still holds for us, *we must enter into the Holy of Holies and not settle along this path*. As you embark on this journey, may this be on the forefront of your mind, and let this be your ultimate goal that; *I must enter the Holy of Holies*. Giving our lives to the Lord is such an exciting thing; the Psalmist talks about restoration to the joy of salvation (Psalm 51:12). Salvation brings so much joy to our souls; however, that is not an end in itself but rather the beginning of this exciting and rewarding journey. It is okay to get started, but pitching our tent permanently along the path should not be an option; neither should we give up. The Lord says, *"But if anyone draws back, my soul has no pleasure in him"* (Hebrews 10:38). Whether you make a u-turn or whether you stop along the way, you have essentially drawn back, and it does not please the Lord. So let us keep moving forward.

The Tabernacle was divided into three sections: namely, the Outer Court (also called the Courtyard), Inner Court (also called the Holy Place), and the Holy of Holies, (called the Most Holy Place). The three sections of the Tabernacle correspond to our triune nature: the Outer Court being our physical body, the Inner Court corresponds to our soul, and the Holy of Holies to our spirit.

The Tabernacle Layout

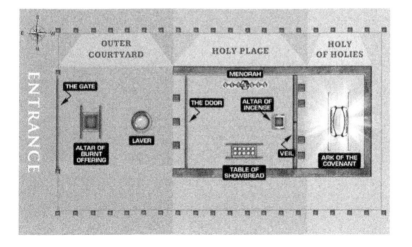

26

Outer Court

The first section of the Tabernacle that we would walk into is the Outer Court. It contained the Bronze Altar (also called the Brazen Altar or Altar of Burnt sacrifices), and the Bronze Laver. The focus in this section of the Tabernacle was on judgement, sacrifice, and cleansing. Everything in the Outer Court was overlaid with or constructed with bronze which is a metal that symbolises judgement. The natural light in this section of the Tabernacle was the source of light.

The first item we would encounter as we enter the Outer Court is the **Bronze Altar**. It was so large and prominent and the priest of God could not bypass the Altar as he entered the Tabernacle. The priest made the animal sacrifices at the Bronze Altar. The Bronze Altar today reveals the redemptive work of Christ. It is the most important part of a Temple. Without the Altar, there is no Tabernacle or Temple, and without the shedding of blood, there is no forgiveness for our sins (Hebrews 9:22), there is no redemption for our souls. It is only through the redeeming blood of Jesus Christ that our sins are covered and we qualify to approach God's Presence.

As we carry on from the Bronze Altar, the next item we would encounter is the **Bronze Laver.** The Bronze Laver is a washbasin that was made of highly polished brass which had been used as mirrors by the women serving at the Temple. The basin was filled with water which the priests used to wash their feet and hands before entering the Holy place, and before ministering at the Bronze Altar. At the Bronze Laver, we are washed and sanctified by His Word and Spirit.

Inner Court

As we move away from the Outer Court and proceed westward into the Tabernacle, we move into the next section, the Inner Court. Only the High Priests could come into this area, and cleansing at the Bronze Laver was a prerequisite before entering the Inner Court. The Inner Court was a quieter, smaller, and less busy place than the Outer Court. There were no windows and hence no natural light in this Holy Place. The source of light was the Menorah, also called the Golden Lampstand.

On the right side of the Inner Court is the **Table of the Showbread**. It was made of acacia wood and overlaid with pure gold. Placed on the table was the Showbread or Bread of the Presence. The Showbread was ever-present on the table and was replaced weekly on the Sabbath. It was laid in two rows, six in a row. Pure frankincense was also placed upon each row.

Opposite the Table of the Showbread on the left side was the **Golden Lampstand**. It was made from one piece of pure gold and had seven branches, three on either side and one in the centre.

The **Golden Altar of Incense** is the last treasure we would encounter in the Holy Place before entering the Holy of Holies. It was made of acacia wood and overlaid with pure gold. Just like the Bronze Altar, the fire of burning coals at this Altar was never allowed to die. Only incense was offered at this Altar and had to arise before God continually. The Golden Altar is a picture of the intercessory work of Christ, our intercessor, who is seated at the right hand of the Father, continually making intercession for us.

The Veil

After the Holy Place, the next and final destination in the Temple is the Holy of Holies. There, however, was a Veil separating the Holy Place from the Holy of Holies. Only the High Priest was allowed access beyond the Veil of separation, once a year, as he entered into the Holy of Holies where God's Presence dwelt. The Veil was made of woven blue, purple, and scarlet thread and fine white linen. It also had cherubim embroidered into it. The veil was a constant reminder to the Israelites that sin makes humanity unfit to be in the Presence of our holy God.

Holy of Holies

The Holy of Holies was the focal point and the ultimate destination of the Tabernacle. In the Holy of Holies was the Ark of the Covenant, which was made of acacia wood, overlaid with pure gold and with specified dimensions. Only the High Priest was allowed to go in there once a year on the Day of Atonement. The Ark of the Covenant contained three items:

- The Tablets with the Ten Commandments.
- The pot of manna.
- Aaron's rod that budded.

The lid for the Ark of the Covenant was the Mercy Seat, also called the Atonement Cover. On it were two cherubim that faced inward towards each other while looking down on the cover, with their wings spreading outward covering the Mercy Seat. This particular area of the Tabernacle contained the very Presence and Power of God. From above the Mercy Seat, between the two cherubim, the Lord would manifest Himself and speak to His Priest.

Tabernacle covering

A fence surrounded the courtyard, and the Tabernacle itself had a covering of four layers of different materials (Exodus 26:1,7,14). Their purpose was generally to cover the Tabernacle just like Christ is our covering. First were curtains of linen of fine quality. Secondly; curtains of goats' hair which signifies atonement (Lev 16:5-28). Thirdly was the covering of ram skins dyed red. A ram was an animal of substitution (Genesis 22:13); Christ became our substitution. Finally, a covering of badger skins was the outermost covering primarily to protect the Tabernacle from adverse weather conditions.

The Four Faces of the Tabernacle

The Tabernacle had four sides synonymous with the faces of Jesus, as seen in the four synoptic gospels. Today the Tabernacle represents us, and we represent Christ. The four sides represent the traits or qualities we all have as children of God, but in varying proportions in each person according to our personalities. As we seek to serve God and fulfil our divine mandates, we must exhibit these traits according to a given situation. As they journeyed through the wilderness, the Israelites camped around four sides of the Tabernacle according to their tribal standards.

- Judah – represented the Lion just as the Gospel of Matthew represented Jesus.
- Ephraim – represented the Ox as represented by the gospel of Mark.
- Reuben – the tribal standard was Man's face represented by the Gospel of Luke.

⊙ Dan – represented the Eagle as seen in the gospel of John.

There are times we need to be bold as a lion and exercise our authority; sometimes we need to roll up our sleeves and get to work like the ox. There are also times we need to fly solo like an eagle, rise with the wind above the storm and soar to a high place where we can see situations from God's vantage point. Sometimes we also need to relate more with people, be compassionate and empathetic. If we ask the Holy Spirit and yield to Him, He will show us what we ought to do in every circumstance.

In the construction of the Tabernacle, the Lord demonstrates the importance of His Holy Temple. Firstly, the Lord was intimately involved in every detail of the structure of the wilderness Temple. As the Lord gave Moses the instruction and specifications at Mount Sinai for the Tabernacle, He commanded him to ensure that all would be made according to the pattern shown to him. The Tabernacle was God-ordained. Secondly, this assignment was not to be carried out by any man. Instead, God divinely chose a craftsman, Bezalel, the son of Uri, whom He filled with the Spirit of God and wisdom to enable him to carry out this great assignment, and other helpers whom He gave understanding to, for this work (Exodus 31:1-9).

Finally, the treasures that God instructed Moses to use in the construction were astonishing in amounts and so very valuable. The gold and silver used are estimated by historians today to be worth multiple millions of dollars at the very least. This value, therefore, means that the Tabernacle or Temple of God is precious, it is WORTHY, and I would like you to hold on to this idea.

This Tabernacle or Temple on earth were copies of the heavenly Temple (Hebrews 9:24). There are two aspects to any Temple for it to be fully functional: firstly, the container or vessel which is the Temple itself, is where God dwells; and secondly, it is essential to point out that the Temple of God is only as important as the **Presence** of God dwells in it.

"The Temple of God is only as important as the
Presence of God dwells in it"

Jerusalem's second Temple, rebuilt by King Herod, was known for its impressive size and architecture; it was magnificent! As Jesus was leaving the Temple on one of the days, one of His disciples said, *"Teacher, look at these magnificent buildings! Look at the impressive stones in the walls"* (Mark 13:1 NLT). The Lord didn't quite share the disciple's excitement and awe of the Temple, and Jesus replied, *"Yes, look at these great buildings. But they will be completely demolished. Not one stone will be left on top of another!" (Mark 13:2 NLT).* Jesus spoke of the judgement coming on the Temple and the Jews in Jerusalem because they had rejected Him as their Messiah and King.

The Lord was also saying that the Temple is insignificant because the Presence of God was not in the Temple. The significance and importance of the Temple is not the beauty of the physical structure but comes from the fact that God is present in it. You could have a beautiful Temple yet without power. Today, the Temple of God is no longer in a specified geographical location where the children of God must go and worship Him; the Bible makes it explicit that we are indeed the Temples of the Living God, we are the carriers of His Presence. The King of the universe has chosen our bodies to be His place of habitation (1 Corinthians 6: 19). Glory be to God! His Power that was once in the Temple of old, believe it or not, is now inside us. His Power lives right inside of us. We are indeed powerhouses because of what we carry!

The Tabernacle pattern was a roadmap that led the children of Israel back into the Presence of God, starting with the redemption of fallen man. The Tabernacle is a structure and a template that God Himself designed, from which we can learn how to approach His Presence, walk with Him, and encounter the Power of His Presence. When we get this revelation and embrace it, it enables us to walk before God in holiness, access His Presence continually, and receive the Power that comes from His Presence, allowing us to do what He calls us to do.

The ultimate Temple is not the Temple made with hands, but the redeemed man, united with Christ (Revelation 21:3, 22-23). You and I, individually and in unity, are the true Temples of God (1 Peter 2:5, Ephesians 2:22). *"Do you not know that your body is the Temple (the very sanctuary) of the Holy Spirit Who lives in you, whom you have received (as a gift) from God? You are not your own"* (1 Corinthians 6:19 AMPC). As we seek the Lord continually, fellowship with Him, and press into His Presence, we get to know Him more, discern His voice, and understand His plan and purpose for our lives. We are then able to fulfil our divine calling. We cannot remain the same in His Presence, we are empowered to do exploits in His name and for His glory.

"But the people who know their God shall be strong and carry out great exploits" (Daniel 11:32)

The Tabernacle gives us, firstly, a picture of God's ultimate plan of salvation. We are saved and covered by the blood of Jesus; with His covering and in His Name, we can approach the Presence of God. As we take a closer look at the

Tabernacle in this book, we will see that Jesus is revealed throughout the Tabernacle. Firstly, the Tabernacle had one entrance which signifies that there is only one way to get to God, and we know today that one way is through our Lord Jesus. He said in the Scripture that *"I am the way, the truth and the life. No one comes to the Father except through Me"* (John 14:6).

Secondly, we will also see that in pretty much all the Tabernacle treasures, Jesus is revealed. Also, interestingly if we were to draw a connecting line to the six objects in the Tabernacle (the Bronze Altar, Bronze Laver, Table of Showbread, Golden Altar, Golden Menorah, and the Ark of Covenant), we see the Cross. Jesus is the fulfilment of the Tabernacle. *"And the Word became flesh and dwelt ('tabernacled' in Greek) among us, and we beheld His glory, the glory as of the only begotten of the Father, full of grace and truth"* (John 1:14). He alone is the way to the Presence of God; like He rightly said in John 14:6.

SAVED TO SERVE

The journey into the Tabernacle would be incomplete without the priests of God. Back in time, Aaron and his sons were the officiated priests serving in the Tabernacle, with Aaron as the High Priest and his sons as the regular priests. In the present age, God has not only made you and I both His Temples but also priests over the Temple of our soul.

The Priestly Garments (Exodus 28:4 – 43)

To minister to the Lord in the Tabernacle, the priests had to clothe themselves in their ministerial garments. The garments were made according to the Lord's specifications. Regular priests wore plain white tunics with a sash and undergarments (shorts). They all served with no shoes on.

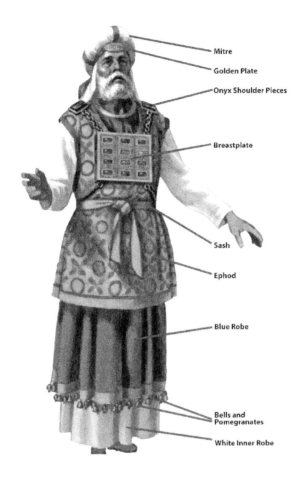

Mitre

Golden Plate

Onyx Shoulder Pieces

Breastplate

Sash

Ephod

Blue Robe

Bells and Pomegranates

White Inner Robe

In addition to regular priestly garments, the High Priest wore an ephod and a breastplate containing precious stones. The ephod was made of gold, blue, purple, and scarlet yarns with finely twisted linen. Under the ephod, the High Priest wore a robe of blue. Golden bells were attached to the hem of the blue robe and were interspaced by pomegranates made from material hung between the bells. On his head, the High

Priest wore a turban also called a mitre of fine linen, and in front of the turban was the golden plate on which was engraved "HOLINESS TO THE LORD," attached by a blue lace ribbon. These were the extra clothes that the High Priest wore on his day-to-day service. On the Day of Atonement, he wore all white: linen robe, sash, hat, and undergarments.

What can we learn from the High Priest's garments?

The High Priest was the only one who had the privilege to enter the Holy of Holies on the Day of Atonement. Throughout the year, he wore unique clothing to distinguish him from the rest, except when he went into the Holy of Holies once a year. There are some pictures painted and lessons we can learn from the High Priest's clothing that we can apply to our lives today to help us serve over God's Temple effectively.

1. **Holiness** – Throughout the year, the High Priest wore a white turban on his head with a plate made of pure gold on the forehead. This indicates that purity and holiness had to be at the forefront of the High Priest's service all year round and not just on the Day of Atonement. All the priests ministered to the Lord in the two outer courts, but the one distinguished with a mark of holiness on his forehead was the only one who entered the very Presence of God. Likewise; we ought to live a holy life if we are to truly encounter and walk

in the Power that comes from the Presence of God. The Bible tells us that without holiness; no one can see God (Hebrews 12:14).

2. **Intercessory work** – The priest carried the names of the children of Israel on both his heart and shoulders, which is significant of intercessory work. On the shoulders of the ephod were two onyx stones, one on either side, and each one had six names of the sons of Israel engraved in it (Exodus 28:9-12), on the breastplate over his heart were also the 12 names of the children of Israel (Exodus 28:29). Today we are all priests over the Temple of God, and intercession is part of our ministry and service to God. We ought to ask the Lord to give us the heart of an intercessor, a heart that loves what He loves and breaks for what breaks His heart so that we stand in the gap and pray that God's will be done on this earth, that His Kingdom may come. The beauty of also praying for others is that when we do, we receive healing and restoration (James 5:16), (Job 42:10).

3. **For Glory and Beauty** – When the Lord instructed Moses about Aaron's garments, He said of the garments that they were **"For Glory and Beauty"** (Exodus 28:2). I believe there were two aspects to the

clothing: the spiritual and the physical side. Glory is the spiritual, and beauty is the physical aspect. As the Word of God and Spirit work together, so do glory and beauty in our service to God. Our outer beauty should mirror our inner beauty of glory.

a. **Glory** is defined as the manifestation of God's Presence as perceived by humans. It is spiritual beauty and has to do with how much of God's Presence we carry within us, which ultimately becomes an outflow of His Spirit that is inside of us as we minister unto others. This glory stems from the quality of the relationship we have with the Lord. I believe the spiritual aspect is also the ministry or anointing for service that would come upon the priest as he put on his clothes which means he is now in office and ready to serve.

b. **Beauty** is the physical aspect of these garments, which is only external and perceived by the eyes of the flesh. I believe it is vital for children of God to dress ourselves in a way that presents ourselves as the beautiful creation of God and His ambassadors on this earth that we are. When we clothe ourselves beautifully, it is a confession of our worth. This is because we carry within us the treasure of His Holy Spirit, and we are so valuable. We honour God when we present ourselves well and we confess to who we belong. If we trust God to use us to glorify His Name, we need to understand that particular doors in this life will open for us because of how we present and carry ourselves.

Though we are not of this world. We are in this world and daily we deal with people of this world who do not have spiritual discernment and are more likely than not going to judge us based on our first impression and external appearance. Can you imagine trying to deliver a message from the Lord to the Queen of England wearing a pair of low-cut jeans and a hoody? Chances are, your foot is not likely to make it through the gate of the palace. Even if you were allowed in, nobody would take you seriously, because your clothes have a language, and they speak even when you are silent.

Queen Esther demonstrated this beautifully. Queen Esther was already married into royalty; therefore, she was royalty by virtue of marriage. She needed to make a request to her husband

King Ahasuerus, but could not speak with the king, as he had not handed her the golden sceptre that was customary and would give her the right to speak with him. First Queen Esther fasted; that is, she put on her spiritual beauty (glory). She then put on her beautiful royal robes (physical beauty), and strategically positioned herself in a place where the king would notice her.

Consequently, Queen Esther got the king's attention and favour; was handed the golden sceptre and presented her request to the king, saving the Jews from perishing. Though the Lord Himself had raised and placed Queen Esther into the palace for such a time and purpose, which was her ministry to save the Jews from perishing, the door to her ministry was not fully opened until she put on her spiritual garment, and garments of beauty (Esther 4:16, Esther 5).

Likewise, you and I are already royalty, as the Bible tells us, but sometimes we do not get the favour we seek with men because we do not present ourselves appropriately. We already have favour with God as His children, but we

43

also need favour with men in this lifetime. You will get a certain favour with men because of the physical covering or robe you present yourself in. Our external beauty should attract and open the doors that God is calling us to go into. His Spirit will be our backing and driving force, enabling us to operate and serve effectively, efficiently, and in the spirit of excellence.

4. **Significance of Colours** – The High Priests' garments had specific colours on them, all of which have a spiritual meaning which we can apply to our lives today:

   a. **Blue** is a heavenly colour that signifies the Holy Spirit. Therefore, we need to ask the Lord to fill us with the oil of His Holy Spirit and for His Spirit to come upon us, which is His anointing for that specific ministry He calls us into if we are to serve Him effectively.

   b. **Scarlet** signifies the blood of Jesus, and it is only through His precious blood that we are worthy to stand before God. So, we ought to cover ourselves in the blood of Jesus, and through the blood of Jesus, we receive forgiveness for our daily trespasses, and by the blood of Jesus, we overcome the schemes of the evil one.

c. **Purple** is a colour that signifies royalty. We are children of the King and a royal priesthood. We ought to reflect this in our conduct, how we speak, and how we present and carry ourselves.

d. **White** is a colour that speaks of purity and holiness. Every area of our lives must reflect this: our bodies, purity of heart and thoughts, our ministries, relationships, etc. Without purity of hands and heart, we cannot ascend into the Presence of God, and without holiness, we cannot see God's face.

5. **Valuable** – The High Priests' clothing was made of finely woven linen, artistically woven and assembled by skilled artists. The breastplate had settings of twelve precious stones. These were explicitly made by gifted artisans whom God had filled with the spirit of wisdom to enable them to make the High Priest's garment. This speaks of quality and worthy material. As children of God, we ought to present ourselves in a manner that

declares our worth and ultimately glorifies God. God selected only fine material for His High Priest to minister before Him. He anointed with wisdom, and gifted artisans to carry out His work. This is very profound and should equally serve us as a standard for presenting ourselves as we stand before God to minister to Him. By so doing, we honour Him and acknowledge that we carry something unique and worthy within us, which is the person of His Holy Spirit.

6. **Fruitfulness –** At the bottom of the priests' robe were pomegranates. Pomegranates are a fruit that has so many seeds. Biblically pomegranates signify fruitfulness, blessing, and prosperity. As the priest is serving God faithfully, just like the anointing of the High Priest flows from his head to the hem of his garment (Psalm 133:3), the results of his service will be fruitfulness, blessing, and prosperity.

Priestly Duties

The priests serving at the Tabernacle had various responsibilities and duties throughout the day and in every Court of the Tabernacle to perform.

The Gates

The Tabernacle had only one entrance, and the Temple in Jerusalem had multiple gates, possibly due to its size. Biblically we know that the gate is an important and prominent place, not only is it a place of access, it is also a place of decision-making and power. Likewise, a gate to the Temple was a crucial point, and if the Temple guards did not take care and the enemy gained access, the Temple could either be destroyed or desecrated. The priests stood there as watchmen. Should the priest fail to fulfil their responsibility or fall asleep, they faced severe punishment.

The priest serving at the entrance to the Tabernacle or Temple was responsible for opening the Temple gates in the morning. They would guard the gates throughout the day and ensure that nothing unclean was allowed access to the Temple that would defile the Temple of God. Should they see an enemy approaching the Temple, they would signal by blowing the trumpet. Thus, the priests at the gate would keep the enemy out and protect the people and Temple. Come to the end of the day, the Temple priests would close the gates at night.

Outer Court

At the **Bronze Altar,** the priests were responsible for performing the animal sacrifices throughout the day. The priest inspected the lamb to ensure it was perfect, with no spots nor blemishes. He would offer a lamb and stand next to the Bronze Altar till the sacrifice was completely burnt. The priest also cleared the ashes to allow a continuous flow of oxygen into the fire.

At the **Bronze Laver**, the priests were required to wash before going into the Holy place or ministering at the Bronze Altar. Before entering the Holy Place, their hands would have been dirty due to blood from sacrifices at the Bronze Altar, and their feet would have been soiled from walking on bare ground. Failure to wash would result in death because God takes holiness seriously (Exodus 30:20).

Inner Court

At the **Table of Showbread,** it was the priests' duty to bake the bread that sat on the table and replace the old bread with fresh loaves every Sabbath**.** They would then eat the previous week's bread, which tradition believed to be still as warm and fresh as when initially placed on the table.

The High Priest was responsible for attending to the **Golden Lampstand**. Every morning and evening, the priest would take a flask of pure olive oil with him into the Holy Place, a pair of scissors and new wicks made from the priests' old garments. The priest would trim any hardened wicks and ensure the wicks were drawing up the oil. He would replace any wicks in the lamps that needed replacing, clean and refill cups that were running low or had run out of fresh oil. He ensured that the light continually burnt and would never die.

At the **Altar of Incense,** the priest would bring coals from the Bronze Altar and add more coals to the Altar of Incense as well as adding more incense. The priest ensured the incense would continually burn and arise before God.

Holy of Holies

The High Priest was allowed into the Holy of Holies once a year, on the Day of Atonement. On this day, no one was allowed to be in the Tabernacle. He would first confess his sins and that of his family on a bull and sacrificed it. Then, he brought in burning coals on a censor from the Bronze Altar and incense in his hands, and took it into the Holy of Holies placing the incense before the Mercy Seat; that is before the Lord as an act of intercession lest he dies. A cloud would arise to cover God's Mercy Seat. He would then sprinkle the Mercy Seat with the blood of the bull and afterward killed the goat for the people's sins, take the goat's blood into the Holy of Holies and sprinkle the Mercy Seat.

With the blood of the bull and goat, he would then atone for the Holy Place anointing the horns of the Altar and all around it, and will do the same in the Outer Court to cleanse it and consecrate from the uncleanness of the Israelites. He would then return to the Outer Court and lay his hands on the head of the second goat; the scapegoat as he confessed the sins of the people over it and sent it off into the wilderness for good. As the blood of animals was never sufficient to completely wipe away the people's sins, the High Priest and the children of Israel carried out this ritual year in and year out.

Modern Day Priest

The High Priest serving in the wilderness Tabernacle is firstly a picture of our Lord Jesus, our High Priest. The High Priest of the Tabernacle wore the ephod which bore the names of each of the Israelite tribes on his breastplate and brought them before God in prayer. Likewise, Jesus' present-day ministry is interceding for us (Romans 8:34).

Today not only are we the living Temples of God, but also the priests of God (1 Peter 2:9). Since the veil of separation that separated us from the Presence of God was torn, we now have greater access to the Presence of God than the High Priest in the wilderness Temple. We can now enter the Presence of God boldly *"by a new and living way which Jesus consecrated for us, through the veil, that is, His flesh"* (Hebrews 10:20).

Thankfully in this dispensation of grace, God has made you and me the priest over His Temple, which is our souls, and we have full access to the Holy of Holies, which is His Presence, not just annually but every day, every moment that you and I choose to enter in. What Power God has bestowed upon us! We do not have to walk with our heads hanging in shame all year round.

The bible records that on the day of the crucifixion of Jesus, the veil was rent from top to bottom to give us access to Him. So, we can enter into the Presence of God today by the spotless blood of the Lamb of God, the perfect sacrifice; what a blessed time to be born and to be alive. We do not have to wait for someone to go in on our behalf. You and I can go in ourselves and encounter Him and the Power of His Presence. What a privilege, glory be to the Lamb of God!

Accessing the Presence of God in the Tabernacle was not a privilege afforded to everybody back in the olden times. Entering the Presence of God was not to be taken casually; there were protocols to be followed in the Tabernacle pathway. You could not just enter in anyhow. Anything unclean would not survive in the Presence of God; the Power of His Presence killed it. Hence the High Priest had to make his sacrifice first on the Day of Atonement, or he would be struck dead in the

Holy of Holies. Thankfully we are in the dispensation of grace; otherwise, we would all have died a long time ago.

It is important to note that the priest did all the required work in the Tabernacle; the sacrificial duties, the washing, the tending of the lamp and the table of Showbread, and the burning of incense. When God was satisfied by the blood and incense, He would then release His glory and fill the Tabernacle. Therefore, we need to remember that, all the duties once carried out by the priests in the Temple, we now have to perform them over our Temples if we are truly to experience the fullness of God's Presence in our souls and lives. *"But you are a chosen generation, a royal priesthood, a holy nation, His own special people, that you may proclaim the praises of Him who called you out of darkness into His marvellous light"* (1 Peter 2:9).

Let the journey begin....

SECTION B

THE JOURNEY BEGINS

ENTER IN

Offering

"Anything you possess that you cannot give to God, or has priority over God, is your idol"

Entering into God's Presence starts with a decision in your heart to seek Him as you offer yourself to Him. Offering ourselves to God means offering our whole being and our substance. I want to present to you this truth: *"Offering precedes the Temple and consequently the encounter".* Before the Tabernacle was constructed, the Israelites generously offered their substance and all the material required to construct the Tabernacle. If we also look at Solomon's Temple, just before entering the main Temple, it had a section in the women's court to the right side where Israelites brought their offering. That was the same place where Jesus commended the widow who gave her two mites (Luke 21:1-4). I believe this is also a picture of us offering our substance to God and offering ourselves to Him physically, mentally, and emotionally.

Giving our substance helps us draw closer to God because where we lay our treasure, our heart will also be there

(Matthew 6:21). There are different types of offerings we can give to God and our level of giving is a reflection of how much we trust Him. When we give to God, we are essentially sowing seeds. The Bible assures us that we will surely reap our harvest accordingly in due season for every seed we sow. The children of Israel offered materials in excess for building the Tabernacle and freely gave their service. Throughout their wilderness journey, they never lacked; God consistently provided all their needs. Likewise, we have to be willing to give of ourselves and do so freely to God. It is God Himself who supplies us with these seeds, after all. *"He who supplies seed to the sower, and bread for food"* (2 Corinthians 9:10).

Below are various forms of offering we ought to give to God:

- ◉ Tithes.
- ◉ Offerings.
- ◉ Giving of ourselves physically through serving God with our gifts and our time.

When we sow seeds, in due season, we reap our harvest, which is our fruit. In that fruit, there is both seed and bread. The seed element is for us to sow back again so that our future harvest is assured. When we fail to do this and eat all our seed, we have essentially consumed our future harvest and provision. A similar analogy would be that of the Dead Sea. The shore of the Dead Sea is at the lowest point of the earth. It receives water from the Jordan river yet has no outlet to maintain a consistent flow of fresh water, so water only escapes by evaporation, leaving behind many salts. Despite the continual water inflow, the Dead Sea is more or less lifeless and unfruitful; plants and animals cannot survive in there as it is too salty, because it has no outlet.

In the fruit that we reap, there is also bread for us to enjoy for ourselves. God wants us to enjoy His blessings. However, we also need to hold lightly to His blessings, be it our jobs, children, and every good thing we receive from Him; otherwise, they become idols and hinder us from serving Him effectively. Nothing in this world is truly ours. We came into this world naked; to the dust, we will return naked (Job 1:21). If we can truly grasp this truth and live by it, we will live a rich and fulfilling life, a life of liberty, peace, and confident trust in the Lord. Our worship and service to God will be more effective and fulfilling. We are ultimately just stewards of all that is in our hands, even our gifts too.

One principle I have learned over the years is that when God gives me a blessing, I give it to Him, sometimes physically and sometimes prayerfully. I give it to Him and not allow it to become an idol. Abraham loved Isaac so much, and God tested Him by asking him to sacrifice the son he loved, the son of promise, unto God. However, the Lord eventually provided

Abraham with the sacrificial lamb just before Abraham slaughtered his son. Spiritually Abraham had sacrificed Isaac to God. He was no longer an idol in Abraham's heart. Soon after this act of obedience, God reaffirmed His blessing to Abraham that was previously promised, and He pronounced even more blessings (Genesis 22:16-18).

I have seen many who loved and served the Lord with all their heart and strength through their struggles. Perhaps they struggled financially or were trusting God for a husband or fruit of the womb. The moment they got their breakthroughs, they were suddenly too busy with family, work, or business to commit to serving the Lord. They no longer had enough time because of the child and husband who needed them. *They took their eyes off the Blesser and gave priority to the blessing; what a tragedy!*

I remember a few years back when the Lord blessed me with a car after going for years without one because I had been in a terrific car accident, and my car was immediately written off by my insurance provider. I was struggling so much financially at that point that the thought of getting a replacement car was just a luxury I could do without. Years later, the Lord began to restore me of my former losses, and suddenly, I was now able to afford a car I fancied. I became so distracted by this car, I was thinking about it daily; every time I opened my eyes in the morning, the first thing I would do was open the door or window, and admire that car. I would think about this car throughout the day and as the last thing before retiring to bed. This futile exercise went on for maybe nearly two weeks until I slowly began feeling distant from the Lord and the Spirit of the Lord convicted me.

I cried out to the Lord in repentance, and in order to lift and cast off this emptiness that was now within me, I took it upon myself to commit to a seven-day fast to recommit myself to Him and also committed my car unto Him. Spiritually I gave my car to the Lord. I felt a release in my spirit, and a release of the car afterward, and my car was no longer an idol. Through this, I also learned the art of holding onto things lightly. You see, it is okay to receive blessings from the Lord and enjoy them because God wants us to enjoy His blessings, but they should never have priority in our lives. The enemy will use that very same thing as a stronghold. I understood this profound truth that anything I possess that has priority over God, or that I cannot give to God, is essentially my idol.

When your heart is set on God, you will find it easier to lay your treasure where your heart is, that is His Kingdom. The beauty is; when you give to God, whatever you give will not be corrupted, and it is never wasted but is a seed that you will receive a harvest for in due season, whether it is the treasure of your money, your time, or gifts. You will also receive eternal rewards.

Reflection:

Do you have any idols in your heart or mind hindering you from giving the Lord first place in your life? Ask the Lord to search you and expose any idols and give Him permission to dethrone them so that He alone can sit on the throne of your life.

The Gates

"A city without walls nor gates is open to destruction"
(Ezekiel 38:11-12)

As mentioned in Section A, the journey into God's Presence in the days of old began by entering through the gate(s). Although the Tabernacle had only one gate to access it, the Temple later built in Jerusalem had multiple gates. The entrance into the Tabernacle would lead firstly into the Outer Court, then the Inner Court, and ultimately the Holy of Holies. Thus, the gate(s) were crucial points concerning the Temple of God. If the priests did not take care, it was a place through which the Temple of God would be susceptible to attack or defilement if the enemy gained access, and could even lead to its destruction.

Priests serving the Temple gate stood there as watchmen. Because of the importance of this point, should they fail to undertake their duty well or fell asleep, they faced great punishment. To recap, the priests carried out the following responsibilities:

- Opening the gates in the morning and closing them in the evening.
- Stopping anything unclean from entering in.
- Closing the gates to deny the enemy access.
- Should they see the enemy approaching, they would blow the trumpet to give warning.

The Bible makes it clear that we are now the Temple of God. *"Do you know that your body is a Temple of the Holy Spirit who is in you, whom you have from God, and you are not your own? For you were bought at a price; therefore, glorify God in your body and in your spirit, which are God's"* (1 Corinthians 6:19-20). The gates to the Temple of our bodies are our five senses: the sense of touch, sight, hearing, feeling, and taste. Like the Tabernacle had three sections: the Outer Court, Inner Court, and the Holy of Holies, we have our body, soul, and spirit. The enemy accesses us physically first through the five senses of our body, penetrating our soul: mind, will, and emotions.

Just like the Temple priests were responsible for guarding and protecting it, it is our responsibility as priests over our Temples to be the watchmen at the gates and keep the enemy out. We must stand to ensure that the Temple is guarded against defilement, attack by the enemy, leading to its destruction. We must diligently guard and examine everything before it goes into the Temple of our bodies and ensure that we will not give the enemy power to access and inhabit in our lives. Biblically, the entrance of a city is considered a place of decision-making and a place also of power. The power lies in our hands to make decisions concerning the gates to our Temple.

I believe we need to be careful what we see, take heed of what we listen to, and ask the Lord to put a guard over our lips. Our mind, heart and emotions are greatly influenced by the things we give access to ourselves through our gates; both consciously and unconsciously. We tend to use our eyes and ears the most and consequently have a greater impact on our lives. Whatever we see and hear frequently will ultimately influence our hearts and mind, and over time, we begin to think similarly, and before we know it, we become likewise. Ralph Waldo Emerson says, "*Sow a thought, and you reap an action; sow* an act, and you reap a habit; sow a habit, and you reap a character; sow a character, and you reap a destiny". You will ultimately become what you think (Proverbs 23:7). Therefore, take heed of what seeds are being sown into your mind.

The Apostle Paul wrote, *"And you* He made alive, *who were dead in trespasses and sins, in which you once walked according to the course of this world, according to the* **prince of the power of the air,** *the spirit who now works in the sons of disobedience"* (Ephesians 2:1-2). From this scripture, we can deduce that Satan rules the air. And in the air we find transmisions including wireless and all kinds of waves and frequencies used to transmit media messages globally. The enemy realises that if he can get our attention through our eyes and ears, he can gain access to the Temples of our bodies and defile us so that we are defiled and without Power.

There is such an exponential rise of media influence in this generation, impacting our beliefs and ultimately our behaviour and character. We should never underestimate the influential power of media in our decision-making and actions. For example, we see the effect of this influence on social media videos or posts going viral, or corresponding increases in sales of a particular product or service when effectively advertised on TV.

Sadly, the media such as TV and social platforms are now filled with immorality, violence, pervasive and sexual nature to the extent that it has become the norm and acceptable for an average believer, thereby searing his conscience. For example, it might not seem like nothing happens when we put on our TV, and a movie of sexual nature pops up for the first time, we probably feel disgusted, and then we put on our television next time, and we see a similar scene, and if we see it a few more times, we become indifferent and unmoved. In the process, we have been groomed, and we become tolerant to sin, and we live with it comfortably in our homes, on TV, the internet, and in magazines.

A story has been told of a frog swimming happily in a pot of water heating on the hob. Though initially cold, the water was gradually heated, and the frog didn't realise it was being cooked until it was too late to jump out and save its skin. The same ought not to be so for us as children of God. As the priest over the Temple of our own body, it is our rightful duty to be selective and diligent of what we let in through the gates of our Temples and to be awake spiritually. We need to examine it all and not give the enemy a passport to take up residence in our Temples.

What we see or hear will ultimately shape our hearts and minds, and eventually, we will produce fruit after what is in us.

Job understood this principle and made this confession "*I have made a covenant with my eyes, not to look lustfully at a young woman*" (Job 31:1 NLT). We can also learn from King David, who failed to guard the gate of his eyes and fell into sin with Bathsheba (2 Samuel 11). He later confessed after he had learned his lesson, "*I will set nothing wicked before my eyes; I hate the work of those who fall away; It shall not cling to me. A perverse heart shall depart from me; I will not know wickedness*" (Psalm 101:3-4).

Even when it comes to music that we listen to on media and allow to minister to our souls, we need to heed what we allow into our Temples. We are in this world; however, we are not of this world. We should not, therefore, be conformed to the things of this world. Another way the enemy tries to defile us is through bad relationships. He strategically places people around us who are not aligned with God's plan and purpose for our lives. These could be friends or other relationships. We can ask God to remove the wrong people from our lives. The enemy can also use family to negatively influence us, often with good intentions. But God will give us wisdom and a spirit of discernment if we ask Him.

God is so good that if we desire to get close to Him and ask Him, He will help us. Sometimes it might not be in the way we expect, but if only we can trust Him and realise that He sees what we do not. He has such a wonderful plan for our lives, so we can learn to surrender to Him. I remember early on in my walk with the Lord, I asked Him to remove any distractions from me so that I could know Him more. To my surprise, I saw the few friends I had pulled away from me one by one; I was left with literally no friends. It was so hard and painful. As if that was not bad enough, my television suddenly stopped working. I tried everything I could to resuscitate it, but to no avail; I just couldn't believe this!

I was in a season where I was struggling so much financially, I was working a limited number of hours, and getting a second job was proving difficult as I was going through a visa battle then, and my passport had been with the home office for a few years. Getting a new television was not an option nor was getting the old one fixed; oh Lord, I was so broke beyond measure! My family was back home in Zimbabwe, I could only call them and speak with them for a limited time as it was pretty expensive, but I couldn't go to see them then. All I was left with was Jesus and faith. In hindsight, if I look back at that season of my life, it was well worth it and so rewarding spiritually, and I am ever so grateful for that dry and lonely season. I learned to spend time and enjoy intimacy with the Lord. He gave me so much peace that was beyond comprehension.

I learned to grow and be rooted in Him every season of the soul and trusted that He could hear me when l spoke with Him. When the going got tough, l learned to cling to Him and trust Him completely. Had l kept my friends, who were not all saved, going back to the wilderness would have been an attractive deal for me. Had my TV still been working, l would have focused on the telly, watched soap after soap, and every unclean thing that would have defiled my soul, causing me to avoid facing the music of the beautiful path to intimacy with the Lord that He was carving out. Being the hoarder that l was then, l kept my dead television with me, and strangely two years later, after l had moved house, for some bizarre reason, l felt prompted to switch it on, lo and behold it was working again after nearly two years! I could not believe my eyes.

But interestingly, something in me had died; l no longer missed anything on telly, l learned to live without it and realised l no longer needed it, and so l gave it away to someone l thought would benefit from it. As l write this book, it is now over eight years since l last owned a working television. My life is just so peaceful without a telly.

Though l do not have a telly, l do ask the Lord for His grace to continually diligently guard the gates of my Temple. I still have to use social media, the internet, and other published articles. Philippians 4:8 is an excellent scripture to meditate on as we seek to keep guard over the gates of our Temples. *"Finally, brethren, whatever things are true, whatever things are noble, whatever things are just, whatever things are pure, whatever things are lovely, whatever things are of good report, if there is any virtue and if there is anything praiseworthy—meditate on these things".*

I have heard some say they have no control over what comes on television, which is true. Still, you do have control over what you continue to watch. If you went into a restaurant and ordered a meal, say the waiter brought you a plate of food and said, "It is on us", then told you that it is some kind of wild dog or poisonous snake on the plate. Would you eat because it has been given to you? I bet not. So likewise, you are in absolute control of what you let through the gates of your Temple. We all have the mandate to be priest over our Temple. If we let the enemy in, we give him a foothold that will hinder us from experiencing the fullness of God's Presence in our lives and will also bring negative consequences which sometimes can be disastrous. Our God is holy, and He requires us to be holy to enter into His Presence.

I believe guarding our gates also requires us to be vigilant about our relationships, who we give access to our lives, and at what level. We need to continually assess these relationships because motives can shift. Our Lord Jesus, the captain of our salvation, set an example for us. Though he had so many followers, He handpicked 12 disciples for Himself, and out of the 12, The Lord further picked 3 to bring into His inner circle; Peter, James, and John, whom He took up the Mountain of Transfiguration. If you do not guard the gates to your Temple, you are just like a city without walls or gates, and you are open to plunder (Ezekiel 38:11-12, Proverbs 25:28). I call to mind Samson, a servant of God, who had a great destiny; his birth was even announced by an angel (Judges 13:3), which was a rare thing. But Samson did not protect the anointing of God upon His life, he let his guard down, and sadly his ministry was cut short; his ministry died on the lap of Delilah, what a shame!

When we get born again, the blood of Jesus cleanses us of our sins. But we need to maintain our purity daily, and we need His grace which enables us to achieve this. We must not rely on our own strength. But first, we need to make a firm decision to glorify God with our bodies and be the priest that we are ordained to be. A great place to start would be with making a covenant with your eyes, like Job did, not to set your eyes on things that defile you, not entertain with your ears what you shouldn't listen to, nor speak words that are ungodly. Next, we need to depend on His Word, to allow it to penetrate and fully permeate through our souls, and always to give His Word the final authority in our lives. Finally, we need to ask for His grace, which will enable us to submit to God, resist the devil's temptations, and watch him flee from us (James 4:7).

Praise

"For our God is great and greatly to be praised
(Psalm 145:3)

As we walk into the Tabernacle through the gates, the Psalmist tells us what manner of attitude we ought to have as we approach God's Presence. The Psalmist declares, *"Enter into His gates with thanksgiving and into His courts with praise. Be thankful to Him,* and *bless His name"* (Psalm 100:4). Jewish tradition says that when the Jews travelled to Jerusalem to the Temple for their annual festivals, they sang Psalms 120 to 134, also known as Songs of Ascent. The city of Jerusalem is set on a hill. I believe that as Jews sang the songs in praise, they could mount the hill more effortlessly, and their souls were lifted. Their eyes were fixed on the one they were to encounter, so they climbed the hill with joy and expectation, and their hearts were fully prepared to encounter Him and receive from Him.

Praise and thanksgiving stir our soul and prepares us to receive from the Lord. Jewish priests are also believed to have sung these Songs of Ascent as they walked up the steps of the Temple in Jerusalem. We praise God for what He has done, what He is doing, and what He is yet to do. When we praise Him, we declare His Power, His greatness, His goodness, and that He is worthy. Praise and thanksgiving empower and cause us to enter His gates; it opens the gates of our heart.

Praising God as we enter His gates lifts us when our soul is cast down and disquieted within us. It prepares our hearts to encounter Him and receive His peace, joy, and strength. Praising Him is also an act of our obedience to His Word (Psalm 150:1). When we praise Him, we take our eyes off our problems and focus them on our great God. As we do so, our view of God is magnified because the things we focus on are exalted in our eyes and consequently our problems are diminished before us as we begin to see them through the eyes of our God. When we praise God, faith begins to rise in our hearts, and this is a vital heart condition in order to receive from the Lord (James 1:6-8). Praising Him is also a weapon of warfare, and our enemies will be defeated. I remember the story of the children of Israel; 13 times, they marched around the walls of Jericho in praise, and they saw victory; the walls of Jericho, which were a stronghold, fell right before their eyes.

I also call to mind a few years back when the Lord gave me a mind-blowing miracle at a time when I felt so helpless in the face of the enemy. I chose to praise the Lord in this situation and declared, "The battle is yours, Lord". I saw a spectacular display of God's power. After studying for a couple of years for one of my professional qualifications and passing all the exams, the final stage was to have a face-to-face interview that tests my professional competency in that field. If passed, then I would be fully qualified and could use all the fancy letters with my names or signature. The company I worked for then agreed to pay the fees for this interview, which was a couple of hundred pounds.

About ten days before this interview, I suddenly fell ill with persistent pain on one side of my body, which did not respond to pain killers. Sleeping was hard; doing day-to-day duties was hard as I was in so much pain and was tired all the time from not sleeping. The last thing I could do was sit up and prepare for this interview. On the day of the interview, though hardly prepared, boycotting it was not an option for various reasons. Fees had been paid, and I also risked being struck off the register of professionals if the interview was not done in a specified time, which meant throwing away all the years of hard work towards my qualification. I had waited for too long for this. In my excruciating pain and weariness, I commanded my soul early in the morning on the day to bless the Lord, and I praised Him.

The journey to the interview centre was about 65 miles long and was yet another battle. There were severe traffic hold-ups due to roadworks and traffic diversions. The satellite navigator could not locate the place when I was just 5 minutes away due to road closures, so l went round and round in circles. I was 27 minutes late, but l called the interviewing centre when l realised l was not going to make it on time, and they were so understanding. When l eventually arrived, l was warmly welcomed by the receptionist who did all the necessary administrative work. The lady who signed me in commended my report and said it was superbly detailed; however, l should expect many questions, which was not particularly good news for me as l was tired and in pain; l smiled back and thanked the lady.

Shortly after this, l was assigned an interviewer, who came to fetch me after reading my report, and we went to a private room for the interview process and sat opposite each other. l had listed my most recent three jobs for my work experience, and the interviewer's first question was asking me to talk him through my experience and duties. I began talking about my first of the three jobs, and in less than a minute, the interviewer suddenly fell asleep right before my eyes! I could not believe what l was seeing; this was so unreal. The man's body had dropped to his right side, and his head was hanging. l could see him breathing, so he was not dead nor had he fainted, l was worried that he might fall from the chair as it did not have armrests, but l could not touch him in case l got accused of inappropriate body contact.

This was unheard of and happened so suddenly; I had hundreds of questions running through my head, and I had to make a quick decision as to what to do. So, I silently prayed, and said "Lord, what do I do?" And He gave me peace that the interviewer was okay. You see, as I was growing up, I was mentally conditioned that if an adult misbehaves, if you want things to be well with you, one of your top strategies is to pretend that nothing happened, you pretend that you did not see anything in order to stay out of trouble. So, with that in mind, I continued talking to the man who was fast asleep about my first job as if the interviewer were awake. When I finished talking about the first job, I paused, waiting for his response.

Eventually, he opened his eyes, they were so heavy with sleep, and he stared right into my eyes but did not utter a word. The Lord then prompted me to start talking about the second job. As I began talking again, the interviewer went straight back to sleep, leaning to one side with his head hanging off the chair. When I finished talking about my second job, I paused, and the same thing happened as before. He opened his sleepy eyes again, and as I began talking about my third job, he went straight back to sleep. The Holy Spirit was clearly in charge, this all became so funny, but I could not laugh as I would get into trouble.

Eventually, when I finished talking about all three jobs, I kept quiet. He then opened his eyes, flicked through my report, asked me no further questions, and then said, "I think you have what it takes to be fully qualified". This whole process lasted just under 10 minutes. So, he took me back to the waiting area and said he was taking my documents to the second assessor for the second interview, and that he would call me when ready. A couple of minutes later, the second interviewer came to fetch me, and we went into one of the booths. This interviewer was quite lively and upbeat.

So, we had a small chat, and we spoke a bit about where I lived and how I travelled to the venue from Oxford. He then went on to ask me, "So how was your first interview? How did you find Mr. X?" In my heart, I heard the scripture "Love covers a multitude of sins," so I smiled calmly at this second interviewer, and I went on to say, "He was good," I even said, "Yes, he was really good," and I smiled back at him. Then he went on to say, "I agree with him too; you have got what it takes to be fully qualified". So, he stretched out his hand to me, and since I perceived he was offering me a handshake, I gave him mine too, and he said, "Congratulations, you are now fully qualified". What! I thought to myself. "Your online portal will be updated later this week, and your certificate will be on its way to you by post," he continued. "Thank you so much," I said, as he asked me to wait in the waiting area for my paperwork.

As I sat there, I saw Mr. X walking across, he looked at me in confusion and with suspicion; I guess he could not make sense of what had transpired and felt a bit embarrassed too. As you can imagine, he was my favourite person that day, so with a big smile on my face, I waved at him and said "Thank you", and he waved back, with a straight face of course. As I received my paperwork, I left the building and began laughing hysterically in the middle of the city streets as I headed back home. I do not know about you, but I am so grateful for this kind of God who orchestrates things in my favour. The Power of praise!

How we praise God usually comes down to our revelation of who He is, our level of faith, and our personalities. In scripture, we see a variety of ways to praise Him ranging from singing, clapping, lifting of hands, dancing, shouting, and playing various musical instruments. How you choose to praise is entirely up to you. I like to dance as I praise the Lord. I am reminded of King David, who when the Spirit of the Lord came upon him, danced before the Lord with all His might (2 Samuel 6:14), so that even his wife Michal despised him in her heart (2 Samuel 6:16). Sometimes our dance or praise might be despised by other people around us, but that is okay; we ought to remember it is not for them, but for the Lord, and therefore we need not lose heart but fix our eyes on the one we are praising.

I also naturally lift my hands and sing as I praise the Lord. I believe that the most important thing is that our praises should be sincere, with a pure heart, given freely and with enthusiasm. I also think that God's praises should be continually in our hearts. We need to cultivate and exercise a heart of gratitude daily. When you go through difficult times or are feeling downcast, I challenge you to look into your life, write down twenty things or as many as you can that you are grateful for, and thank God for them, name them one by one and see what that does to your heart.

So let us enter His gates with praise and thanksgiving. For our God is great and greatly to be praised (Psalm 145:3).

Prayer:

Heavenly Father, I thank You that You have made me and entrusted me to be a priest over the Temple of my soul, Your very sanctuary. Today, I ask for the grace to guard over this Temple diligently and the grace to protect the gates to this Temple. Let grace abound to me, oh Lord, to be diligent to scrutinise everything that seeks access to this holy Temple and grant me a discerning spirit to be able to discern between good and evil. Strengthen me daily to watch and pray so that I will not be caught off guard.

Thank You, Lord, that when I draw near to You, You will draw near to me too. As I seek to draw near to You in praise, I pray that my praises will be with a sincere heart and not just lip service. Great and greatly to be praised are You Lord. Grant me a generous spirit that I will offer You my substance, time, and gifts in service, and to be a faithful steward. Amen.

LAY IT ON THE ALTAR

*"I have been crucified with Christ, and it is no longer I
who live, but Christ lives in me" (Galatians 2:20)*

A s we walk through the entrance into the Tabernacle, the
first section we walk into is the Outer Court. The Outer
Court of the Tabernacle corresponds to our physical body. Just
like the Outer Court of the Tabernacle was the furthest from
the Presence of God, so is our flesh. The source of light in the
Outer Court was the natural light, the sun that can be seen with
our eyes of the flesh. The Outer Court was also a place of much
activity and noise related to the noise from sacrificial animals
fighting in resistance, crying when being slaughtered against
their will, burning of sacrifices, and all the activities happening
in there. All Israelites had access to this part of the Tabernacle.

In the Outer Court, the first item we encounter is the
Bronze Altar. The Bronze Altar was constructed according to
specific instructions as seen below, given to Moses by God
(Exodus 27:1-8):

- It was made of acacia wood and overlaid with bronze.

- It was five cubits wide by five cubits long with a height of three cubits.

- It had horns on its four corners, which were one piece with the Altar.

- It contained a bronze grate where the priest would lay the sacrifice.

- It had four bronze rings at its corners. Poles made of acacia wood and overlaid with bronze were inserted into the rings on the two sides of the Altar to carry and transport it.

The Bronze Altar

In addition, bronze utensils were made to be used at the Altar: pans, shovels, basins, forks, and firepans. The Bronze Altar, or Altar of Burnt Offering was a place of sacrifice and the most crucial part of building a Temple. Without an Altar and the shedding of blood, there was no functioning Temple. Interestingly, Mount Moriah is where King Solomon built a Temple for God, and in the same place, the Second Temple was also built. It was a place associated with sacrifice. Abraham encountered the High Priest Melchizedek around this area of Mount Moriah (Genesis 14:18-20) and honoured him by paying the very first tithe that we find in Scripture. When tested by God years later to sacrifice the son he loved so much; the son of promise, Abraham returned to Mount Moriah with Isaac to offer him unto the Lord as a sacrifice (Genesis 22). It is also believed that it was near Mount Moriah where the Lord Himself was crucified.

The fire on the Bronze Altar was not allowed to die (Leviticus 6:13); it had to burn continuously. After Adam's fall into sin, all humanity became corrupted and were now sinful. God's holiness requires a blood sacrifice to cover sin. God instituted blood sacrifices as an offering to cover for the people's sins so they could come into His Presence. Without blood sacrifices, there would have been no need for the Tabernacle. All activities in the Tabernacle were centred on blood sacrifices. *"For the life of the flesh is in the blood, and I have given it to you upon the Altar to make atonement for your souls, for it is the blood that makes atonement for the soul"* (Leviticus 17:11).

Let's dig for the treasures in the Bronze Altar.

1. **Salvation** – The Bronze Altar is a picture of salvation. It is the first item you encountered in the Tabernacle; the priest could not proceed into the Tabernacle without first stopping at the Bronze Altar. Today it is the Cross of Jesus Christ that we have to encounter first as we seek to come into the Presence of the Lord. The Bronze Altar is very much a type of cross of our Lord Jesus Christ. God's requirement for a blood sacrifice to atone for our sins still stands today, and thankfully, we have the redeeming blood of our Lord Jesus. The blood sacrifices in the Tabernacle signified man's need for God's mercy to be able to enter into God's Presence.

   The priests performed blood sacrifices repeatedly as animal blood sacrifices could never completely take away the people's sins. However, when Jesus was crucified, God's requirement for blood sacrifices was fulfilled because He is the perfect lamb of God, a lamb without blemish or spot (1 Peter 1:18-19). Jesus was the final atonement for our sins. Thankfully through the Lord's sacrificial death on the Cross, He took away our sin once and for all. He purchased our salvation and reconciled us to the Father. So, by accepting Him as our Lord and Saviour, we are receiving His atoning blood and are covered by it, which makes us welcomed into the family of God and qualifies us to be in the very Presence of God before His throne. There is no other name under heaven given among men by which we must be saved, but the name of Jesus (Acts 4:12)

2. **Jesus is the way** – The Bronze Altar was the largest piece of furniture in the Tabernacle and was too prominent to be missed. It pointed to Jesus as the Way of salvation from judgement. The priest could not minister in the Tabernacle until he had gone to the Altar first for sacrifice, signifying its importance. Jesus became our sin and burnt offering. The precious blood that He shed for us atones for our sins today. Likewise, we cannot bypass Jesus to go to God. Jesus said, *"I am the way, the truth, and the life, no one comes to the Father but through Me"* (John 14:6). The reason for the blood sacrifices performed was to make atonement for the Israelites' sins and to lead them to God. This blood sacrifice principle still holds today. Without blood sacrifice, there is no atonement for our iniquities;

without Jesus' blood, we cannot enter the Presence of our Holy God. So, to worship God with our service, which is the ministry we are called into, we need Jesus. He is the way. We can only qualify to stand before God and serve Him through faith in the name of Jesus and His righteousness. Jesus is the way and the door to the Presence of God.

3. **A place of Judgement** – the Bronze Altar was overlaid with bronze, and bronze utensils were made for use with it. Bronze is a metal that signifies judgement. The Altar placed in the Tabernacle reminds God's people of the consequences of sin, which is death. But because God is merciful, He required that His people take an innocent animal and sacrifice it in their place for their sin. When we look to the Cross of Calvary today, this is a place where the judgement of a holy God fell upon our sins. Our Lord Jesus Christ bore our sins as they were laid upon Him on that cursed tree. Scripture records that: *"He made Him who knew no sin to be sin for us, that we might become the righteousness of God in Him"* (2 Corinthians 5:21). Like in the Old Testament, when the High Priest pronounced the people's sins on a scapegoat, our Lord Jesus took our sins upon Him; He became our scapegoat. All our

sins and curses were laid upon Him (Galatians 3:13). So, we are free indeed because the Son has set us free. We are liberated to serve God and to fulfil every divine assignment. He redeemed us from the curse.

4. **A place of redemption –** When our Lord Jesus Christ was crucified on the Cross of Calvary, one of the things He accomplished for us was redemption. To redeem is to buy back. Jesus is our Redeemer. The evil powers had enslaved us; we were not of God, so we essentially belonged to the dark kingdom because we are the devil's if we are not His. The Lord purchased us back with His precious blood into His Kingdom where we formerly belonged until the fall of man in the Garden of Eden. Scripture says: "*Knowing that you were not redeemed with corruptible things, like silver or gold, from your aimless conduct received by tradition from your fathers, but with the precious blood of Christ, as of a lamb without blemish and without spot*" (1 Peter 1:18-19). So, when we come to light of this truth and believe it with our hearts, we must confess it; we must proclaim our redemption.

Quite often, when we try to move forward in our calling, we will find ourselves struggling in specific areas or feeling stuck; it sometimes feels as if some invisible powers are holding us back and fighting our progress, sometimes we even see patterns running in the family such as generational curses or bloodline issues. It might even be sickness when you try to advance in life. I remember a time in the past that whenever I tried to work on a business I was being led into, I would feel ill and lethargic whenever I tried to advance and was quick to agree with the enemy that I was sick and quickly jumped into bed to rest. Strangely it was happening either at a specific time or when I tried to do this work.

I remember one of the nights when I lay in bed feeling so poorly, I saw a messenger of God speaking to me in a dream, and it was so vivid, "The Lord said I have healed you completely". He said this with such a firm conviction leaving no room for doubt, but when I woke up, that was not the case; I was still frail and poorly. But I chose to believe the Lord's report and began to proclaim my redemption from sickness or any disease boldly. I had an appointment later in the day to see the doctor. He carried out every test he could imagine, every blood test he could think of, and a few days later, I got my results, and there was absolutely nothing wrong with me. I realised then that this was not actually sickness I was battling with but some invisible spiritual powers that were at work.

Proclaiming my redemption and declaring what the Word of God says about my health was the gamechanger. By the blood of the Lamb and the word of my testimony, I overcame (Rev 12:11). I mastered the enemy's tactics. Whenever I see him creeping around because he is relentless, instead of jumping into bed for a nap, I would get into prayer, resist him and command him to flee from me because he no longer has any legal ground. I would then carry on with my work. Beloved, the devil has no power over you and I, he no longer has legal ground over us (John 14.30), but we need to proclaim our redemption boldly. We believe the Word of God with our hearts, but we must also confess it with our mouths unto manifestation (Romans 10:9-10).

5. **We are so valuable** – At the Bronze Altar, we see the great exchange that took place; blood in place of man's life. In the olden times, it was the life of an animal that could redeem the children of God, only temporarily. When the Lord Jesus Christ died for our sins, we ascertained our great value according to the Scripture (1 Peter 1:18-19). Though gold and silver are known to

be pricy, they are worthless and perishable compared to the blood of our Lord Jesus that redeemed us. Therefore, you and I are so valuable, and we are worthy; we were redeemed at such a high price.

6. **Jesus is our refuge and safety** – The Altar had four horns, one in each corner. Among other things, horns were also a place where you could hold onto and find security. David's son, Adonijah, went into the Temple and laid hold of the horns on the Altar as he tried to escape the wrath of Solomon, the new king of Israel. Solomon spared him as he clinged onto the horns of the Altar and asked for mercy. The horns of the Altar were sprinkled with the blood of the sacrificial sin offering. So, when Adonijah grabbed hold of the horns of the Altar, he was firstly acknowledging himself as a sinner and also pleading for mercy and laying claim of the forgiveness offered by the sacrifice (1 Kings 1:50).

And today, our forgiveness is in Christ alone, and it is on the basis of what He did over 2,000 years ago on the Cross of Calvary. We need to lay hold of our crucified Saviour. Jesus has our backs covered. When we are fearful, overwhelmed, or under threat, we can run to Jesus. He is our place of refuge and our place of safety. *"The Name of the Lord is a strong tower; the righteous run to it and are safe"* (Proverbs 18:10).

7. **A place of forgiveness** – The Bronze Altar was also a place of forgiveness. When we accept Jesus as our Lord and Saviour, we are cleansed of our sins by the blood of Jesus. As Jesus taught His disciples to pray, He said we needed to repent of our daily trespasses. So, we know that more often than not, we are likely to sin daily. This could be a sin of commission, omission and even our thoughts. Sin separates us from God, from His Presence. *"But your iniquities have separated you from your God; and your sins have hidden His face from you so that He will not hear"* (Isaiah 59:2).

Whenever the Israelites sinned against God, they would bring their sin offering to the Altar, with their hearts heavy with the weight of their sin, and present it to the priest. After seeing their sacrifice presented and accepted by our Holy God, they would walk away in liberty, assured of God's forgiveness for their sins. The innocent animal instead would bear their penalty.

But today, it is through the blood of Jesus that our sins are forgiven. *"In Him, we have redemption through His blood, the forgiveness of sins, according to the riches of His grace"*

(Ephesians 1:7). Without shedding of blood, there is no redemption for our souls. *"And according to the Law almost all things are purified with blood, and without shedding of blood there is no remission"* (Hebrews 9:22). He is our sacrifice and our priest who offers the offering on the Altar. So, we need to come to Him daily and repent of our sins, ask Him to forgive our daily trespasses, and we receive our forgiveness through faith in Him. Any unconfessed sin hinders us from experiencing the Power of His Presence. *"Who may ascend into the hill of the Lord? Or who may stand in His holy place? He who has clean hands and a pure heart, who has not lifted up his soul to an idol, nor sworn deceitfully"* (Psalm 24:3-4). We need to claim daily the Power of His blood over our lives as we repent for our daily trespasses. And when we ask for forgiveness, we need to receive it and believe with our hearts that God has forgiven us.

8. **We are the burnt offering** – The Bronze Altar, also called "the Altar of Burnt Offering," emphasised the burnt offering, a sacrifice of devotion and worship. When the Israelites presented the burnt offering, it represented their worship of God. As we come to God, we also offer up our bodies as a living sacrifice at the Bronze Altar. Apostle Paul says that a sacrifice that is

holy and pleasing to God, that *"this is your true and proper worship"* (Romans 12:1-2 NIV). As we dedicate ourselves to God as an acceptable offering to Him, he consumes our hearts and sanctifies us by His fire. Our God is holy, and for us to draw near to Him, sin must die. We need to lay ourselves wholly on the Altar and allow the fire on the Altar to consume every part of our being that defiles us and does not bring Him glory. We need to get to a place where we can boldly confess like Apostle Paul said, *"I have been crucified with Christ, and it is no longer I who live, but Christ lives in me, and the life which I now live in the flesh I live by faith in the Son of God, who loved me and gave Himself up for me"* (Galatians 2:20).

If we are to move forward from here, we also need to ask the Lord to search our hearts for any idols that may compete for our attention and hinder us from giving Him the priority in our lives. The priest inspected the lamb at the Bronze Altar and made sure it had no spots or blemishes. It had to be a perfect lamb. We need to ask the Lord to search our hearts, to purify our hearts with His holy fire. *"Create in me a clean heart, O God, and renew a right spirit within me"* (KJV Psalm 51:10). As we come to the Altar, we lay down all our burdens and cares and give them to the Lord. We let go of bitterness, unforgiveness, anger, fornication, adultery, and everything that may defile us. We lay on the Altar every weight that will easily ensnare us so that we may run our race for God's glory and with endurance unto the finishing line (Hebrews 12:1). *Your race is that which God is calling you to do. It could be your ministry, business, or career.*

At the Altar, we sacrifice our time, gifts, and money as the Spirit of God leads us. A sacrifice is different from an offering; in simplistic terms, an offering is something you give out of your abundance, and a sacrifice is something that is costly to you. So, when we give a sacrifice, we are not giving a surplus that we do not care about or won't notice if we lose. King David understood this principle and insisted on paying for all the items he needed to build the Lord's Altar, which Arunah had offered to give him for free. King David said, *"I will not sacrifice to the Lord my God burnt offerings that cost me nothing"* (2 Samuel 24:24 NIV). *If our gifts are meaningless to us, surely we cannot expect them to be meaningful to God.* In Hebrew, the word *"sacrifice"* is *"korban"*, it means "to draw near to". The reason for Tabernacle sacrifices was to draw the children of Israel near to

God. So, when we present sacrifices to God, we are drawn further into His Presence.

9. **Keep the fire burning** – Amongst other duties, the priest was responsible for clearing the Altar of the previous day's ashes from the burnt sacrifices. The fire on the Altar was to burn continuously, so removing the ashes was necessary as a build up of ashes would hinder oxygen from getting through to the fire and extinguish the flame. In our personal lives, the ashes represent anything that extinguishes the flame of His fire in our lives, hindering us from accessing the fullness of His Presence such as disappointment, offence, resentment, anger, unforgiveness, or bitterness of soul. So, when we come to the Altar in repentance, we need to let go and lay all our burdens on the Altar and receive healing and forgiveness. When we are whole, the flame of our hearts keeps burning and burns the brightest. As the priest of our own Temples, let us continually clear the ashes in our lives so we can keep our fire burning brightly for Jesus.

When you have laid all on the Altar, you receive cleansing for your sins and trespasses and healing for your soul. You will experience peace, joy, and freedom that allows you to move forward on this journey towards the Presence of God. God delivered the children of Israel from Egypt for a purpose. I believe God likewise has also delivered you and I for a purpose, not so that we should be content with salvation and stop here. He did not take us out of bondage only to just leave us here, so we need to move forward and lay hold of that which Christ has also laid hold of us. He who began a good thing in us is faithful to bring it to fruition (Philippians 1:6). So let us keep moving forward.

Prayer:

Heavenly Father, I thank You that the blood of Jesus cleanses me of my sins, through faith in my Lord Jesus, I am in right standing with You, I am the righteousness of God. I pray this day that You forgive me my trespasses. Any sin I have committed unknowingly, uncover it that I may repent. Help me to live a life worthy of Your calling and bear fruits worthy of repentance. As I willingly give my body to You, laying it on the Altar, I lay every sin and every burden that may easily beset me, that I may run my race to the finishing line for Your glory. Purify and refine me with Your Holy fire. In Jesus mighty name, I pray. Amen.

SET APART

"Who may ascend into the hill of the LORD? Or who may stand in His holy place? He who has clean hands and a pure heart, who has not lifted up his soul to an idol, nor sworn deceitfully" (Psalm 24: 3-4)

Moving on away from the Bronze Altar and proceeding further into the Tabernacle, the next thing we encounter in the Tabernacle's Outer Court is a washbasin called the Bronze Laver. It was positioned between the Bronze Altar and the Inner Court. This piece was built as follows (Exodus 30:18-21):

- It was made of bronze, both the Laver and its base.
- The Laver was of highly polished brass, which was reflective like mirrors. These were the mirrors of the women who served at the entrance to the Tent of Meeting.
- It would contain water where the priests would wash their hands and feet before ministering to the Lord in the Holy Place.
- No specific dimensions were given for its construction.

The Bronze Laver

God instructed Moses that the priests, Aaron the High Priest and his sons, would wash their hands and feet before entering the Holy Place and when they came to minister at the Bronze Altar. Failure to do so would result in the death of the priests; this signified how God took this cleansing seriously before ministration (Exodus 30:19-21).

Let us dig for the wealth in the Bronze Laver:

1. **Baptism and Consecration** – After its completion, the Tabernacle and its vessels were anointed and consecrated. Then God instructed Moses to bring Aaron the High Priest, and his sons to the door of the

Holy Place and to wash them with the water. Afterward, he would put holy garments on them, anoint and consecrate them so that they can minister to God as His priests, "...*for their anointing shall surely be an everlasting priesthood throughout their generations*" (Exodus 40:11-15). This kind of washing was done once, and it was final. This is a picture of baptism and consecration. To consecrate is to set apart as holy, to make or declare sacred for God's use. It can also be defined as to dedicate or ordain. When Jesus was baptised by John the Baptist, God declared Him, by His Spirit, His Son in whom He was well pleased (Mark 1:11). At the appointed time, He stepped into His ministry. Interestingly Aaron's sons were washed at the door rather than inside the Holy Place signifying that this is a necessary step before progressing into the Presence of God.

2. **Cleansing** – Ephesians 5:26-27 tells us that we are sanctified and cleansed "with the washing of the water by the Word", that we might be presented before the Lord as a glorious church, without spot or blemish but as a holy bride. As we feed ourselves with the Word of God, it is the water of His Word that washes over us and cleanses us. Therefore, the Bronze Laver is a

picture of our cleansing by the Word of God, and it is also a picture of Jesus Himself, He is "the Word" (John 1:1-2). All the priests had to stop here each time before proceeding to the Inner Court or to minister at the Bronze Altar. God is holy, and His law required that the priests washed their hands which were contaminated with blood from undertaking daily sacrifices at the Bronze Altar, and their feet that would have been dirty from walking on the bare ground. Failure to observe this law resulted in the death of the priest.

Our hands signify our work or ministry; we need to serve God in purity. Scripture tells us that to ascend the hill of the Lord, which is His Temple, or to qualify to stand in His Holy Place, we must have clean hands and a pure heart (Psalm 24:3-4). The priests also washed their feet before entering the Holy Place. Feet represent our walk, character and conduct, and where we go or hang around. As we carry out our service to God, we need to walk that holy walk and in cleanliness before God. Where we go and hang around is a matter of concern to God and can either maintain our purity or defile us.

Ministering to God requires cleansing regularly as it is possible to be contaminated along the path or process of our service. Sometimes we are not even aware of our errors and need cleansing from our unknown and presumptuous sins and even our secret faults (Psalms 19:12-13). As the priests approached the Holy Place, they would have ministered at the Bronze Altar, yet God still required them to wash their hands and feet at the Bronze Laver.

In our service to God, we need regular cleansing and washing of water by the Word if we are to render effective and fruitful service unto the Lord, or we risk being contaminated, which negatively affects our spiritual life. So, it is paramount that we stop first at the Bronze Laver before ministering to God. This cleansing applies to every area of our lives, whether serving in church, in business, our workplaces, in the community and in our homes.

Our external man reflects our inner man. More often than not, this inner cleansing will manifest physically or externally as our inner and outer beings are connected and begin to come into alignment. It can be friends or relationships being removed sometimes through a seemingly natural and seamless process but sometimes through an involuntary and painful process.

I remember a time early on in my walk with the Lord; His Spirit led me to do a wardrobe decluttering. At first thought, this sounded easy and exciting. But when I got deep into it, being a hoarder that I was then, I struggled so much to let go of my clothes. It was the first time in possibly at least seven years and it was such an emotional experience. There was sadness, crying, jumping back into the bin at times, and taking back what I had thrown away. Eventually, when I had finished, I felt so light, lighter than I had felt in such a long time. I realised there was some internal cleansing that had taken place at the same time.

When we hold on to certain things, we hold on to sentiments, good or bad; we cling on to our past, which can hinder us from moving forward or growing and being fruitful. When we fill our lives with things from the past, physically, emotionally, and spiritually, this can hinder blessings, or hinder new things from flowing into our lives because we are clogged up and full. We have no room to receive more and fresh things if we have clutter in our lives. The Dead Sea is at the lowest point on earth, it always receives water from all the other rivers, yet there is no life in it just like its name; it is so salty, and water cannot flow out to maintain its freshness. We become like the Dead Sea and cease to be fruitful when we allow clutter; when our outward channels are blocked.

3. **Sanctification** – To sanctify is to make holy, consecrate and set aside for God's use. It is the continual and progressive process in the life of a believer; moving away from sin and heading toward righteousness. It is a progressive process of becoming more like Christ. When you become a believer, you are justified (at the Bronze Altar by the blood of Jesus). Then the Spirit of God begins the process of sanctification to separate you from sin continually. This sanctification is the work of the Word which washes us. Jesus said, *"Sanctify them by Your truth, Your word is truth"* (John 17:17).

But we also know this water of His Word signifies His Holy Spirit. Jesus said *"the Words that I speak to you are Spirit, and they are life"* (John 6:63). By the washing of the water of the Word and Spirit, we are progressively cleansed and set apart as vessels of honour fit for God's use. *"But in a great house, there are not only vessels of gold and silver, but also of wood and clay, some for honour and some for dishonour. Therefore, if anyone cleanses himself from the latter, he will be a vessel for honour, sanctified and useful for the Master, prepared for every good work"* (2 Timothy 2:20-21).

For us to approach God's Presence and serve Him, we need to be consecrated and sanctified. Like in the Mount Sinai encounter, the Presence of God was at this mountain, and Israelites who approached God had to be consecrated, sanctified, and had to wash their clothes (Exodus 19:10,14). When we are sanctified before God and serve Him in purity, we can see His Power moving in our lives. Joshua spoke to the children of Israel just before crossing the river Jordan into the Land of Promise, and he said, *"Sanctify yourselves, for tomorrow the Lord will do wonders among you"* (Joshua 3:5). Sure enough, the children of Israel saw the move of God's power when the Lord granted them resounding victory over the city of Jericho, and they saw the great walls of the city tumbling down. When we are contaminated, we cannot see victory in our lives.

To their surprise, soon after the walls of Jericho fell, the children of Israel went to fight the army of Ai, which was almost insignificant as it was so small in number, the Israelites were shamefully defeated. When Joshua cried out to the Lord, the Lord said: *Get up, sanctify the people and say, "Sanctify yourselves for tomorrow, because thus says the Lord God of Israel: 'There is an accursed thing in your midst, O Israel; you cannot stand before your enemies until you take away the accursed thing from among you'"* (Joshua 7:13). The children of Israel had sinned against the Lord (Joshua 7:11).

4. **The mirror of His Word** – The Bronze Laver was covered with reflective mirrors, which allowed the priests to see themselves as they washed. As the truth of God's Word cleanses us, l believe God wants us to look at ourselves through the mirror and light of His Word, to look intently into the mirror of His Word. He wants us to see ourselves as He sees us, that is through the lens of His Word so that we can begin to walk in that Word, live out that Word, and not walk away only to forget the Word and do our own thing but to be guided and to allow the Word of God to have the final authority in our lives.

Looking into the mirror of His Word also will enable us to see where we have drifted from the truth so that we can take corrective action. The book of James refers to this as "the perfect law of liberty". *"For if anyone is a hearer of the word and not a doer, he is like a man observing his natural face in a mirror: for he observes himself, goes away and forgets what kind of man he was. But he who looks into the perfect law of liberty and continues in it and is not a forgetful hearer but a doer of the work, this one will be blessed in what he does"* (James 1:23-25).

We ought to wash daily and to look in the mirror of God's Word continually as our gates (our senses) are exposed to contamination from things of this world, through all kinds of media, words we hear, or things we see around us. Sometimes we do not realise it as it might be so subtle in the beginning, but the more we are exposed, the seeds begin to grow as they are nurtured and take root in us. Before we know it; we are thoroughly contaminated, hence the need to be vigilant and allow the truth of His Word to wash us and the reflection to correct us. When we look into the mirror of His Word, it can discern the intents of our hearts, our thoughts, and any wrong motives within us.

His Word is able to expose and cut away anything ungodly within us. *"For the Word of God is living and powerful, and sharper than any two-edged sword, piercing even to the division of soul and spirit, and of joints and marrow, and is a discerner of the thoughts and intents of the heart"* (Hebrews 4:12). As we continue to look into the mirror of this Word, which is the Lord Himself, it will constantly transform us into the light of His image, and we become more and more like Him. *"But we all, with unveiled face, beholding as in a mirror the glory of the Lord, are being transformed into the same image from glory to glory, just as by the Spirit of the Lord"* (2 Corinthians 3:18).

5. **Judgement** – The Laver was made of bronze which signifies judgement. Cleansing ourselves at the Bronze Laver involves self-judgement in light of the Word of God as we see our reflection in the mirror. The idea being that when we examine and judge ourselves, we take corrective action so that we will not be condemned together with the world (1 Corinthians 11:27-32). Paul once warned the church concerning the Lord's Supper that we ought to examine (judge) ourselves first before partaking of the communion in an unworthy manner. He warned of some people who did not do this and received the judgement of God; some fell sick, some became weak, and some even died.

6. **No limits** – Interestingly, with most Treasures of the Tabernacle, God specified the measurements, but not so for the Bronze Laver; no dimensions were given. I believe this says we can have as much of God's Word as we would like. There is no limit to how often and how much of God's Word we can allow to wash over

us. Washing from contamination, for every child of God, is a continuous process which should last for as long as we are here in this fallen world. The fact that the Bronze Laver is significant as it also means that there is no limit to how much revelation and how deep we can go with the Word of God, which is why it is quite possible to get a new and more profound revelation from the same scripture each time we go to read with an open heart and mind.

7. **Press in** – The Bronze Laver was placed just before we move in to the Inner Court, implying that if we are to move on to experience the Presence of God and minister in whatever way He is calling us to, we need His Word to cleanse us and sanctify us. To move from a place of repentance and salvation to a deeper and more meaningful relationship with the Lord, we need His Word. So let us not get content with salvation, but hunger for an encounter with the Power of His Presence as we feed ourselves daily with His Word and allow it to wash and sanctify us. Let us not look at ourselves in the mirror of His Word and walk away, forgetting what we looked like and not do anything about it. Let us not be content to pitch our tents and camp in the Outer Court but be diligent in doing what

it takes to move into the Inner Court. Let us not be satisfied with an Outer Court relationship with the Lord. Let us not be satisfied with pure milk but desire the meat of His Word.

This quote by William S Burroughs resonates well with me, and he says, "When you stop growing, you start dying". If we stay in the Outer Court for too long, there is a danger of growing complacent; our hearts grow cold and become hardened. Let us then press on to perfection. "...*Let us draw near with a sincere heart in full assurance of faith, having our hearts sprinkled clean from an evil conscience and our bodies washed with pure water. Let us hold fast the confession of our hope without wavering, for He who has promised is faithful*" (Hebrews 10:22-23 NASB 1995). Staying in the Outer Court is just as bad as giving up, because God wants us to ultimately enter His Presence and step up to do what He calls us to do. He says in His Word, "*But if anyone draws back, my soul has no pleasure in Him*", (Hebrews 10:38). Let us be willing to pay the price so we can ultimately get into the fullness of His Presence, be empowered, and fulfil God's purpose for our lives while we are here on this earth.

Coming into the Outer Court is a necessary step to get into the Presence of God. Still, He does not want us to settle there, *"Therefore leaving the principles of the doctrine of Christ, let us go on unto perfection; not laying again the foundation of repentance from dead works, and of faith toward God" (Hebrews 6:1).* Beloved, God is waiting and longing for you to come into His Presence. Will you dare press in and find out what He has in store for you?

Prayer

Dear Lord, I thank You that You are Jehovah M'kaddesh; You are my sanctifier. I pray this day that You would give me hunger daily for Your Word and grace to study it diligently. As I study Your Word, let the water of it wash over my soul. Sanctify me wholly, my body, my soul, and spirit. Put a guard over my lips Lord that I may be blameless before You, Holy God. Season my speech with salt, and I pray that my words may impart grace to the hearers. As I look into the mirror of Your Word, please show me where I may have gone astray and grant me the willpower to be a doer of Your Word. Preserve me as a vessel of honour, fit for the master's use in and out of season, in Jesus' mighty name. Amen.

SECTION C

PRESS IN

OUR DAILY BREAD

As we move away from the Outer Court and press into His Presence, we find ourselves in the Inner Court. The treasures in there were either made of gold or of acacia wood and overlaid with gold. Each one of three treasures in the Inner Court had a specific purpose and meaning. They give us insight that helps us transition from salvation to transformation of our souls so that we might draw nearer to the Lord and have a closer fellowship with Him.

The three treasures were: the Golden Lampstand, also known as the Menorah; the Table of Showbread, also called the Table of the Bread of Presence; and the Altar of Incense, also called the Golden Altar. The Inner Court correlates to the soul of man. The three objects found in the Inner Court correlate to specific aspects of our soul. The mind corresponds to the Menorah, and the light of the Menorah lights up our mind. Our will corresponds to the Altar of Incense, where we freely give our prayers, intercession, and worship. Our emotions relate to the Bread of the Presence, and they need to be ever in the Presence of the Lord.

Interestingly, the size of the Holy Place was much smaller in comparison to the Outer Court. There were fewer activities for the priest to carry out in this section of the Tabernacle. It was generally a place of quiet, communion, and worship, unlike the Outer Court, which was busy and noisy. It gives a picture that for us to draw closer to the Lord, we need to drift away from our activity of the flesh, from mental noise to the quietness of the soul, and be in a position where we can tune in to the frequency of His Holy Spirit, to hear His voice, the still small voice. Intimacy with the Lord requires isolation. It often means physically isolating ourselves. Still, sometimes this isolation can even be during corporate worship when our soul is quiet and aligned with the Holy Spirit, where we can sense His Presence strongly and discern His voice. However, this is learned or cultivated by consistently spending time with the Lord and getting to know Him more.

"Abide in Me and I in you ...for without Me you can do nothing" (John 15:4-5)

As mentioned above, when we walk into the Inner Court, we find the Table of Showbread located on the right-hand side of the Inner Court with the Table made as follows (Exodus 25:23-30):

⊙ It was made of acacia wood, overlaid with pure gold and with a gold moulding all around.

- It was two cubits long (equivalent to 3 feet), a cubit wide and a cubit and a half high.

- It had a frame, a handbreadth wide with a gold moulding all around it.

- It had four rings of gold placed at the four corners of its four legs.

- The rings were close to the frame and were used as holders for the poles to carry the table.

- The poles were made of acacia wood and overlaid with gold.

The Table of Showbread

Additionally, dishes, pans, pitchers, and bowls for the pouring at the table, were all made of gold. The Lord further instructed Moses to set the Showbread, also called the Bread of the Presence, on the table before Him always. Like the Ark of the Covenant, the table was handled and moved only with poles, emphasising its holy status.

The priests were responsible for baking the Showbread, which consisted of 12 small, flat round loaves. They made the Showbread using the finest wheat, moulded it, and baked it. They then placed the twelve loaves of bread on the table, arranged six loaves on either side with frankincense sprinkled on each row. The two stacks of bread sat side by side, and the priests were responsible for replacing it every Sabbath when they would eat the old loaves. The loaves of bread were considered holy and were eaten only by the priests. Throughout the duration of the bread on the table, it is believed that the bread stayed as warm and as fresh as when the priests had initially placed it on the table.

What lessons can we draw from the Table of the Presence?

As I pointed out earlier, the Inner Court of the Tabernacle corresponds to our soul. Our emotions precisely correspond to the Table of the Showbread.

- ◉ The Table of the Showbread was overlaid with pure gold and was not to be touched with hands but carried with golden poles, which highlight its holiness. This signifies that for us to enjoy fellowship with the Lord, we need to come in holiness.

⊙ The Showbread was always before the Lord and kept fresh. Similarly, we need to keep our emotions before the Lord continually, and they are always kept fresh, nourished, and aligned with the truth of His Word.

⊙ The priests replaced the bread every week on the Sabbath, and this is a picture of our need to rededicate our inner man to the Lord regularly.

⊙ The bread was surrounded with frankincense which represents worship. When we worship God, our emotions are kept pure and in alignment with God's will.

Our daily bread.

The Showbread is a picture of the Word of God. God provided manna to the Israelites daily. It strengthened, nourished and sustained them. Every morning, the children of Israel had to go out into the wilderness to receive the manna for the day. They were allowed to collect just enough manna for the day. If they tried to collect more than enough for the day, it would breed worms and rot (Exodus 16:20). When the disciples asked Jesus to teach them to pray, He taught them that they ought to ask for their "Daily Bread" (Matthew 6:11). God wants us to depend totally on Him, to go to Him daily for our bread which is His Word, and from which we receive strength for our inner man and nourishment. He knows everything we need daily, and He wants us to continually fellowship with Him through His Word and not just when the need arises or when we have spare time. We need to make time for Him daily because we need this bread daily.

If we go for long without this bread, we will slowly grow weak spiritually and become malnourished. Without this daily bread, we become vulnerable to physical, mental, emotional attacks, and become easy prey for the enemy. Just like in the physical, if we stopped eating food, we become physically weak and malnourished, our immune system becomes compromised, and we are susceptible to attack. Eventually, our spiritual life is compromised, and we become unfruitful. Jesus said that *"Man shall not live by bread alone, but by every word that proceeds from the mouth of God"* (Matthew 4:4). So, we need to feed our inner man with His Word daily; it is necessary to be fruitful in every area of our lives that God is calling us into.

The bread of life & the bread of heaven.

The Showbread is also a picture of Jesus. We know from the book of John that Jesus is "the Word". *"In the beginning was the Word, and the Word was with God, and the Word was God. He was in the beginning with God"* (John 1:1-2). Jesus said, *"I am* the bread of life" (John 6:48). *"I am the living bread which came down from heaven. If anyone eats of this bread, he will live forever: and the bread that I shall give is My flesh, which I shall give for the life of the world"* (John 6:50-51). Jesus taught us through His disciples as they partook of His body through communion at the Last Passover meal: "…And He took bread, gave thanks and broke it and gave it to them saying, *'This is my body which is given for you; do this in remembrance of me'"* (Luke 22:19). So, whenever we are taking communion, we acknowledge the significance of the bread, that it represents Jesus. And as we take and eat it, we are feeding on His body, the bread of heaven, which gives us spiritual life, nourishment, strength to enable us to do His will.

The bread of the covenant.

This was also a constant reminder of God's eternal covenant with His people, the Israelites. The twelve loaves represented their tribes. Today all believers have been grafted into the family of God, Jew or Gentile. When the Israelites took the Passover bread, it had no leaven. Leaven represents sin, and so this bread without sin is our Lord Jesus. When Jesus had the Passover meal with His disciples, He said, *"Take, eat, this is My body"* (Matthew 26:26). Jesus said to His disciples, *"This is My body which is given for you; do this in remembrance of me"* (Luke 22:19). So, today, the table is where we remember what the Lord achieved for us and where we have communion with Him.

Table fellowship signifies friendship and also covenant relationship. God wanted to be in the midst of His people to rule over them and have friendship and fellowship with them. So, when we take this bread, we remember Him, we recommit ourselves to Him and His will, our friendship and covenant are strengthened, and so are we spiritually.

Why feed yourself on the Word?

In our pursuit to do the will of God and fulfil our divine purposes, studying and knowing the Word of God is vital and brings about so many benefits to enable us to fulfil every assignment. We need not just to know the Word of God but to meditate on it day and night so that we may have good success (Joshua 1:8). Meditating on the Word of God is more than just reading it; but it means to think on, to ponder, to dissect from different angles. I am reminded of and would like to compare this to a cow ruminating. Rumination or cud-chewing is the process by which the cow regurgitates previously consumed feed and chews it further. This physical process allows a breakdown of particle size into smaller sizes and improves the digestion rate which allows for higher levels of feed intake, thus greater nutrient input.

We, therefore, need to feed on Him daily, dissect the Word as we meditate on it, and apply it to our lives. That way, we will be able to bear much fruit. One thing that also captivates my mind is that Joshua 1:8 talks about having "**good success**", which means there is also "bad success". I believe that success is truly good when it is aligned with God's Word, His will, and plan for our lives. When we seek Him, He aligns our gifts and desires with His plan and purposes for our lives and gives us the desires of our hearts. He then blesses the work of our hands with a blessing that makes us rich, fulfils us, and adds no sorrow to the blessing (Proverbs 10:22).

Below are more benefits of studying and meditating on the Word of God:

- When we feed ourselves with the Word of God, His Word continually **renews** our minds so that we do not conform to worldly things, and this continual renewal brings **transformation** to our minds. As a result, we can discern between good and evil and what is acceptable before God and His perfect will for our lives (Romans 12:2).

- In the pursuit of our divine assignments, the Word of God makes our path clearer so we can see clearly and not stumble in our path. It also illuminates our minds and gives us clarity. The Word is a **light** (Psalm 119:105).

- When we have the Word of God in us, to enables us to pray according to God's will, which is in His Word, we receive **answered prayer**. Jesus said when we abide in Him, and His Word abides in us, we will ask what we desire, and He will do it for us (John 15:7).

- Source of **nourishment and fruitfulness**. A branch cannot bear fruit in itself unless it abides in the vine. Jesus (the Word) is the vine, and we are the branches, and without Him, we can do nothing (John 15:4-5).

- Our **faith is strengthened**. If we confess the Word of God, which is in line with what we are trusting Him for, when we hear this Word over and over, we believe and start acting in accordance with this truth (Romans 10:17).

- **Discerner of our thoughts**. The Word of God can discern the thoughts and intents of our hearts. As we look into the mirror of the Word, we can see a reflection of our thoughts, the intents of our hearts, and our hidden motives (Hebrews 4:12). With the water of the Word, we can then wash ourselves clean and be sanctified.

- When we go astray or are side-tracked, the Word **corrects** and **instructs** us so that we can return to the right path and be thoroughly equipped for every good work of the Lord (2 Timothy 3:16-17).

- If we heed the word of God, we receive **knowledge** and **understanding** in whatever area or field God is calling us to serve in. *"For the* Lord *gives wisdom; from* His *mouth come knowledge and understanding"* (Proverbs 2:6).

⦿ The Word of God is a source of **wisdom**. We can receive wisdom beyond our years. The Word of God gives us even more understanding than our teachers (Psalm 19:7b, 119:99).

⦿ Time and again on our course we get disappointed or discouraged. But the Word of God is a source of **joy** and we find **encouragement** in it (Psalm 19:8a).

⦿ It gives us **freedom**. When we abide in His Word, the truth of His Word will liberate us from all bondages: mental, physical, and spiritual, as we continually meditate on the Word of God so that it takes root in us and we are free to advance and do what God is calling us to do (John 8:31-32).

⦿ It **revives** our soul (Psalm 19:7a NLT, Psalm 119:25).

⦿ It is a source of **healing** and **deliverance** (Psalm 107:20).

⦿ When we delight in His Word, just like trees planted by the rivers of water, we become fruitful at the appointed time, and the works of our hands prosper (Psalm 1:1-3), we receive **blessing and prosperity**.

⦿ **His Word equips us for warfare.** The Word of God is likened to a helmet that gives us protection and a sword of the Spirit to fight spiritual battles (Ephesians 6:17).

⊙ Builds up **resistance to temptation.** When His Word is in our hearts, it gives us the ability to recognise temptations that are contrary to the Word and gives us the willpower to resist (Psalm 119:11, Luke 4:4).

⊙ Gives us **boldness.** The enemy will surely rise up and plot against us time and again, but when we have the Word, we are not shaken but meditate on it and confess the truth of the Word over our life (Psalm 119:23).

⊙ The Word **strengthens** us physically (1 Samuel 28:22), **and strengthens** our hearts (Psalm 104:15b).

When we have studied this Word, we need to be doers of it; we need to believe it with our hearts and confess it over our lives until we see a manifestation.

PRAYER

Dear Lord Jesus, You are the bread of life, and You are my daily bread. Give me the hunger to feed on Your Word daily and let this word heal, nourish, strengthen and revive my soul. Align my emotions with the truth of Your Word as I keep them before You. As I study and meditate on Your Word, grant me wisdom and understanding for what You are calling me to do, boldness to rise up that I may have good success. Thank You Lord, that through Your Word I can resist every temptation of the enemy set to derail me from Your wonderful plan and purpose for my life, and Your Word is a weapon of warfare by which I prevail over the evil one. Amen.

LIGHT OF THE WORLD

"I am the light of the world. He who follows Me shall not walk in darkness, but will have the light of life"
(John 8:12).

"You are the light of the world. A city that is set on a hill cannot be hidden" (Matthew 5:14-15).

Moving away from the Table of the Showbread, straight across from it on the Tabernacle's left side, we find the Golden Lampstand. The Lampstand had seven branches, one in the centre and three on either side. Each branch has some specific decorations which I will explore further in this chapter. The Lampstand had seven lamps arranged so that they give light in front of it. It was made of pure gold as were its utensils: wick-trimmers and their trays. The pure gold signifying its purely divine nature, and the word "pure" also meaning they were ritually clean. All decorations and the branch itself were of one piece (Exodus 25:31-40).

The Golden Lampstand

Let's mine for the gold in the Golden Lampstand.

The Light of The World

The Golden Lampstand was the only light source in the Inner Court, which would otherwise have been dark without this light, and the priest would not have been able to see as he ministered in the Holy Place. The single light source is a picture of our Lord Jesus, who is our light and the light of the world. The positioning of the Golden Lampstand in the Inner Court indicates the light that could be seen as a child of God when we look to Christ as a believer who has been saved at the Bronze Altar and pressed past the Outer Court. This light in the Inner Court implies that it is quite possible to be a child of God, and yet the only light you can discern is the natural light or that you live a carnal life so to speak and walk in darkness, unless you press past the Outer Court into the Inner Court where Jesus becomes your light, *"…God is light and in Him is no darkness at all"* (1 John 1:5).

The Lord Jesus said, *"I am the light of the world. He who follows me will not walk in darkness but will have the light of life"* (John 8:12). When Jesus came to live in Capernaum, in the regions of Zebulun and Naphtali, beyond Jordan and Galilee, the Bible confirms this as the prophecy of prophet Isaiah being fulfilled when he said: *"The people who sat in darkness have seen a great light, and upon those who sat in the region and shadow of death, light has dawned"* (Matthew 4:16). This indeed confirms that Jesus is undoubtedly the light of the world. The true light which gives light to every man coming into the world (John 1:9). So, when we look to Him, He becomes our light, and we cannot walk in darkness.

The Golden Lampstand is also a picture of you and I as Jesus' disciples. He said, *"You are the light of the world. A city that is set on a hill cannot be hidden, nor do they light a lamp and put it under a basket, but on the Lampstand, and it gives light to all who are in the house"* (Matthew 5:14-15). God has called all His children to be a light in this dark world. When we surrender to Him, He fills us with the light of His glory, then we can fulfil our divine purpose as we begin to shine and radiate on this earth with His light so that those who are around us and are in darkness will see this light, which will point them on the way to the great Master, the Captain of our salvation. Therefore, let us shine our light in this world unapologetically because God did not call us to hide under a basket.

The Light of His Word

The Golden Lampstand was made from one piece of pure gold, with a total of **seven** branches: one in the centre and three on either side. In addition, there were specifications regarding the decorations moulded into each branch.

- Each of the six branches contained **3 bowls or cups** in the form of an almond blossom for holding the oil and wicks, and each bowl had an **ornamental knob** and a **flower**. So, in total, there were nine decorations moulded into each outer branch (**3x3**).
- The centre branch contained **4 bowls or cups** in the form of flowers for holding the oil and wicks, and each bowl had an **ornamental knob** and a **flower**. So, in total, there were **12** decorations moulded into the centre branch (**4x3**).

So, if we add all the decorations on the left branches, we get **27**(9x3). When we add the decorations of the centre branch **12**(4x3) we get **39 decorations** which corresponds to the **Old**

The Power in His Presence

Testament number of books. If we also add all the decorations on the right branch (9x3), we get **27**, corresponding to the **New Testament** number of books. In total, we have **66 (39+27)** decorations, corresponding to the number of books in the Bible. What then does this say about the Golden Lampstand? The word of God is indeed our source of light. The Psalmist wrote, *"Your word is a lamp to my feet and a light to my path"* (Psalm 119:105). When we have the Word in us, we do not walk in darkness; the light of His Word lights up our mind and illuminates our path. We have clarity in our walk with God and clarity of mind. His Word gives us direction and lights up our way to see as we walk so that we do not stumble. It is also a discerner of our hearts and brings to light wrong and secret motives we might hold.

We also see that the Golden Lampstand had **seven** branches. The number seven is a number that biblically signifies perfection; this then tells us that the word of God is perfect and complete. *"The words of the Lord are pure words, like silver tried in a furnace of earth, Purified seven times"* (Psalm 12:6). Everything we need, we find it in the word of God. So, we need to study the whole counsel as Paul exhorted the Ephesian elders to do (Acts 20:20,27). The seven branches also represent the seven spirits of God, according to Isaiah 11:2. The Word of God is indeed complete. Complete enough to illuminate our minds and give us wisdom, even wisdom to the simple. The

Word of God is a source of understanding. When we are flooded with the Word of God which is Spirit, our Menorah or mind, so to speak, is lit up.

Keep the Oil Flowing

One of the duties of the High Priest was to attend to the **Golden Lampstand**. *"Then the Lord spoke to Moses, saying 'Command the children of Israel that they bring to you pure oil of pressed olives for the light, to make the lamps burn continually. Outside the veil of the Testimony, in the Tabernacle of meeting, Aaron shall be in charge of it from evening until morning before the Lord continually; it shall be a statute forever in your generations. He shall be in charge of lamps on the pure Gold Lampstand before the Lord continually'"* (Leviticus 24:1-4).

Daily the priest trimmed the wicks of any clogged or dead ends. As we are now the priest of God over our Temples, it is our responsibility to check our soul for any clogged or dead wicks that block the free flow of the oil of the Holy Spirit in our lives. Daily we are exposed consciously and unconsciously to negative media, words that can block the free flow of the Holy Spirit in our lives. We need to keep our souls in check and ensure our lamps are still burning brightly for the Lord.

In the section on the Outer Court, l spoke about guarding your gates and ensuring that nothing defiled comes into the

Temple. Sometimes we let things slip in, perhaps because we doze off, our lifestyles become too busy, we lose sight of our priorities and forget to guard our gates, or we are just caught off guard. In practical terms these things could be wrong actions or words we are exposed to, leading to lust, bitterness, anger, strife, and disappointment. It is the same things that gain access to the Temple of our body which will desensitise us, block our wicks, and hinder the free flow of the oil of the Holy Spirit from flowing through us and our fire then begins to suffocate and eventually will die if no corrective action is taken.

Cares for the things of this world, all sorts of idols that we may have, and prayerlessness blocks our wicks, so to speak, and we become less sensitive and less receptive to the things of the Spirit. Sin too has the same effect, our hearts become hardened, and we cannot draw close to the Lord when we desire to because sin separates us from the Lord, and when our hearts are hardened, the oil of His Holy Spirit cannot flow freely through us, and we cannot sense His Presence. Just like the priests of old, it is our responsibility to diligently go into the inner court of our souls and trim the clogged and dead ends daily. How do we do that? We confess and repent of our sins. We ask The Lord to search our hearts and uproot every planting that is not of Him.

Keep the Lamp Burning

The Lord asked Moses to command the Israelites to bring clear oil for the light in order to keep them burning continually (Leviticus 24:1). The Lampstand gave light, but it required oil to keep it burning. The fuel source for the Menorah was the olive oil which the High Priest replenished regularly and ensured it did not run out. This oil signifies the Holy Spirit in us, which empowers us and illuminates our minds. Just like it was the priest's job to ensure that the oil never ran out, it is our responsibility to ensure we are filled by the oil of His Holy Spirit, as we spend meaningful time with the Lord.

When we have the Holy Spirit in us, it illuminates our minds. We also receive a revelation of the Word of God. Two disciples walked with Jesus on the road to Emmaus, but they did not recognise Him (Luke 24:13-16). Likewise, it is possible to walk with Jesus and not recognise Him, and it is possible to read His Word and yet still be without understanding.

Just like the priest checked and ensured that the Golden Lampstand was refilled with olive oil daily, we need to go before the Lord daily and ask Him to fill us with the oil of His Holy Spirit. We have to recognise and accept that we need a refill, and take action. Jesus said that those who hunger and thirst for righteousness shall be filled (Matthew 5:6). We, therefore, go to the Father when we recognise our need, we ask for fresh oil, and that He relights our fire, and ask that our flame is reignited with His continually burning fire.

The Source of Our Life

The Menorah had a shape like the Tree of Life in the Garden of Eden, signifying life. Jesus said, *"The Words that I speak to you are spirit, and they are life"* (John 6:63b). Jesus is the Word and our source of life. Just like the tree in the Garden of Eden, which was to show Adam and Eve that God was the source of their life. When they sinned, they were cut off from the Tree of Life and they were driven further from God's Presence. When we are cut off from the Lord's Presence, who is our source of life, we cannot bear fruit in our lives. The cups and flowers of the Menorah were depicted as almonds which also symbolise resurrection. As we are filled with the oil of His Holy Spirit and receive the light of His Word, our flowers begin to bud and resurrect, our gifts of the Spirit begin stirring up and start to come alive. When we are connected to Him, the true vine, and abide in Him, we can't help but bear so much fruit.

Light Without Limit

Just like the Bronze Laver, God did not specify the measurements for the Golden Lampstand. I believe this also says there is no limit to how much of God's light we can have in us. There is no limit to how often and how much of the light of His Word we can take in. We can have as much of the oil of His Holy Spirit as we can contain within us. As long as we are willing and open to receive, we can be continuously filled, receive revelation upon revelation of His Word, consistently overflow, be a light, and always walk in the light. We can always move from glory to glory. We, therefore, need to ask the Lord to enlarge our capacity to receive from Him because God has so much to give us.

PRAYER

Lord Jesus, You are the light of the world. I pray that You illuminate my mind with Your light so that I will not stumble in the darkness of this world. Your Word is a lamp to my feet and a light to my path. As I feed my soul on Your Word continually, and as I embark on my divine assignment, let the light of Your Word give me clarity and light up my path that I may see the way. I do pray for fresh oil on my head today, the oil of Your Holy Spirit. As I continually seek You in Your Word, fill my cup constantly with Your oil so that I may be a light in this world, and I do pray that my light will never be put out but continually burn. Set my soul on fire Lord, fire that can never be quenched. Amen.

AT THE FEET OF JESUS

"Let my prayer be set before You as incense, the lifting up of my hands as the evening sacrifice"
(Psalm 141:2).

As we move away from the Golden Lampstand toward the Holy of Holies, just before the veil that separated the Inner Court from the Holy of Holies, we find the third and last treasure; the Altar of Incense, also called the Golden Altar. It was constructed as follows (Exodus 30:1-6):

- It was made of acacia wood and had four horns on top, which were all one piece.
- Its dimensions were one-cubit length, one cubit wide (square-shaped), and two cubits high.
- Its top, sides, all around, and horns were overlaid with pure gold.
- It had a moulding of gold all around it, and under the moulding on both sides were two gold rings.
- Two poles made of acacia wood, overlaid with gold, were placed in the rings for carrying the Golden Altar.

The Golden Altar was explicitly for burning incense, and the Lord gave Moses the recipe for the incense composition.

The Golden Altar

The Incense Recipe.

"And the Lord said to Moses: 'Take sweet spices, stacte and onycha and galbanum, and pure frankincense with these sweet spices; there shall be equal amounts of each. You shall make of these an incense, a compound according to the art of the perfumer, salted, pure, and holy. And you shall beat some of it very fine and put some of it before the Testimony in the Tabernacle of meeting where I will meet with you. It shall be most holy to you. But as for the incense which you shall make, you shall not make any for yourselves, according to its composition. It shall be to you holy for the

Lord. *Whoever makes any like it, to smell it, he shall be cut off from his people"* (Exodus 30:34-38). The recipe for the incense was not to be replicated. It was not allowed for private or any other use except for worshipping God in the Temple. It was unique, and God Himself copyrighted it.

No strange offering or other offering was to be burnt, offered, or poured on this Altar. The Golden Altar was placed before the veil, which was just before the Holy of Holies. Aaron was required to burn sweet incense on the Altar every morning when he tended the lamps and also in the evening at twilight. With a censer (a pan with a handle on it), hot burning coal was taken from the burnt offering with blood, which was placed on the Altar, and the High Priest added incense to it, and a beautiful smell went up into the Holy of Holies. This incense had to burn before the Lord continually.

Let us uncover the treasures hidden in the Golden Lampstand:

Prayer and Intercession.

Incense is primarily a picture of prayer and intercession, our prayer, and that of Jesus our intercessor. The Psalmist also wrote, *"Let my prayer be set before You as incense, the lifting up of my hands as the evening sacrifice"* (Psalm 141:2). We also see that while the children of Israel were in the wilderness, God sent a plague to destroy them as they had turned against Moses and Aaron, and they began murmuring. Instead of running away, Moses and Aaron fell to their faces and began interceding on behalf of the people. Moses then sent Aaron to immediately get fire and incense from the Altar and run with it into the midst of the people. Aaron responded by immediate obedience, and as soon as he took the incense into the midst of the people to make atonement for them, the plague stopped (Numbers 16:41-48). The Golden Altar was the closest of all treasures in the Tabernacle to the Holy of Holies. Its positioning does signify that prayer and intercession bring us much closer to the fullness of the Presence of the Lord.

Jesus our Intercessor.

The High Priest would, daily, offer incense morning and evening. Aaron being the High Priest then, was a type of Jesus, who is our High Priest today. Aaron offered up the incense, a type of prayer and intercession; this is a picture of our Lord Jesus making intercession on our behalf. *"But He, because He continues forever, has an unchangeable priesthood. Therefore, He is also able to save to the uttermost those who come to God through Him, since He always lives to make intercession for them"* (Hebrews 7:24-25). Jesus ascended to the heavenly throne and is seated on the Father's right hand, continuously interceding on our behalf (Romans 8:34). Jesus said to His disciples, which is essentially what you and I are today, *"I pray for them. I do not pray for the world but for those whom You have given me, for they are Yours. And all mine are Yours, and Yours are mine, and I am glorified in them"* (John 17:9-10). It is the King himself always praying for us. If we look at the top of the Golden Altar, we see a crown on top of the Altar, which is symbolic of this kingship.

Crushed and Transformed.

As the Lord was instructing Moses how to make the incense, He said of the ingredients, *"And you shall beat some of it very fine, and put some of it before the Testimony in the Tabernacle of meeting"* (Exodus 30:36a). The crushing reminds us of our Lord Jesus, who was "crushed on our behalf" (Isaiah 53: 4-7), and His end was glorious. He became the sweet-smelling aroma that was acceptable before God. We, too, can be transformed if we allow the challenges, tests, crushing, and fires we go through in life to change us. If we would not give up and hold on tightly unto the Lord with unwavering faith, trusting that He has such a wonderful plan for our lives and yield to the process, we would produce a fine, pure, and sweet-smelling sacrifice, acceptable before the Lord. Just like our Lord Jesus Christ, we would also have a glorious ending.

Jesus is our Righteousness and Mediator.

Incense also represents Christ as our righteousness and mediator. The High Priest would take coals from the Bronze Altar where blood would have been sprinkled. Through this shed blood and sacrifice on the Bronze Altar, worship at the Golden Altar was made possible, and incense was acceptable before God. On the Day of Atonement, the Altar of Incense was purified by the sprinkling of blood, which made prayers acceptable before God. Today we need to be covered in the blood of Jesus and go in the name of Jesus as we stand before God in prayer for our prayers to be acceptable before God. Jesus is our righteousness and our mediator.

Incense represents our worship of God.

"Then another angel, having a golden censer, came and stood at the Altar. He was given much incense, that he should offer it with the prayers of all the saints upon the Golden Altar which was before the throne. And the smoke of the incense, with the prayers of the saints, ascended before God from the angel's hand" (Revelation 8:3-4). The priest would bring burning coals on a censer, into the Holy Place, and pour out the incense on the Altar. This incense would then produce a delightful aroma. The incense is also a picture of our hearts' offering when the blood of Jesus forgives our sins, and we freely express our love and worship to God, which is like a

sweet-smelling fragrance, pleasing before God and acceptable to Him.

The Altar of Incense is a picture of a surrendered heart from which we are offering up our prayers to God and our worship. We take our eyes off ourselves; nothing at this point matters, and we give our soul entirely, our inner being regardless of our circumstances. The Altar of Incense was connected to the Bronze Altar; coals from the Bronze Altar were continually taken to the Golden Altar. That means as we offer up our worship to God, we are also offering up our body as a living sacrifice. This idea was a continuous thing that the fire should never go out at the Altar, neither should the incense ever stop burning, which primarily represents our prayers and also our worship; they should never cease to arise before God.

Lifestyle of Worship.

Just as incense from the Golden Altar had to arise continually before God, so does our worship. We ought to pray without ceasing (1Thessalonians 5:17). Continually offering prayer or worship does not mean being constantly on our knees; it is more about maintaining an attitude of readiness for prayer and worship, in and out of season. It is about continual awareness of the Presence of the Lord, acknowledging Him, and remaining in dialogue with Him. It is a lifestyle whereby we invite the Lord into our day-to-day activities such as our jobs, businesses, finances, and relationships. We invite Him into our errands such as shopping, holidays, travel, hobbies, and even in our silence. Simply put, we invite Him in to be the Lord of every area of our lives.

God wants us to live a lifestyle of worship, and He wants us to worship Him from the very depths of our hearts freely. Interestingly, salt is one of the ingredients used to make incense. Salt is generally used as a preservative, a flavour enhancer, and a purifier. So likewise, as we worship the Lord, we need to worship Him with pure hearts and have no hidden motives and we need to preserve this purity of heart to be a flavour-enhancer to this earth, the salt of the world. The Golden Altar was overlaid with "pure" gold which also emphasises this purity of heart if our worship is to be acceptable before God.

When we live a lifestyle of worship, there is no longer a divide between secular and sacred in our lives. Our will and hearts are totally surrendered to the Lord. Mary of Magdala is a woman in the Bible whose worship inspires me so much. Before Mary had an encounter with Jesus, she was possessed with seven demons, I guess that is a complete set of demons you can think of, and the Lord delivered her from them all. Since then, Mary Magdalene made a firm decision to serve the Lord with all her heart and her substance. She followed Jesus in service all the way from the North of Israel in Magdala to Jerusalem. When Jesus was crucified, Mary was right there at the foot of the cross. When Jesus was resurrected from the grave, she was one of the very first few people Jesus showed Himself to, and Jesus sent Mary of Magdala to the 12 apostles, "but go to My brethren and say to *them, I am ascending to my Father and your Father* and to My God and your God" (John 20:17b). Because of her surrendered and fully devoted heart, the Lord commissioned Mary Magdalene to go to the apostles. So, she became "an apostle to the apostles", Hallelujah!

But what is it to worship?

To worship is to acknowledge and ascribe worth to someone or something. From a biblical perspective, when we worship God, we acknowledge that He is our King and the Lord of our lives. This revelation results in living our lives in light of this truth.

- In the original Greek, the word for worship is "*proskuneo,*" which means **kneeling** or **prostration** to do homage (to one), whether to express respect or to make supplication.
- The word worship in old Hebrew translates to "*shachah.*" And it means to **bow down**, or **prostrate** oneself before a monarch or superior in homage.

When we kneel, bow down or lie prostrate, this is a result of our worship. But also bear in mind that one can still be on their knees physically, yet actually be standing in their heart; there is no reverence for God whatsoever in their hearts in this circumstance. What does this mean then? **"Worship is more of a heart attitude than it is our posture"**. Outward expressions may help reinforce or stir up our worship, but ultimately, it is our hearts He wants.

We worship God for who He is. When we worship Him, we commune with Him at the deepest level of our spirit. The Psalmist said, "deep calls unto deep," (Psalm 42:7), which is spirit to Spirit. Everything about our lives is holy and sacred to God. The words we speak, our jobs or businesses, how we spend our time, our conduct, how we present ourselves, how we spend our money even the jokes we entertain. God wants us to worship Him freely, from the depths of our souls. Sometimes our worship can be spontaneous but waiting, or lingering can also be necessary, just like the incense is gradually burnt to produce that sweet-smelling aroma that rises and is acceptable before His throne.

The Veil.

After the Holy place, our next and final destination would be the Holy of Holies. However, there was a veil separating the Holy Place from the Holy of Holies. Only the High Priest was allowed access beyond the veil once a year into the Holy of Holies, where God's Presence dwelt. But thankfully, when Jesus our High Priest was crucified, the veil was torn from top to bottom, giving us unlimited access to the Presence of God so that we can access Him whenever we wish. *"Therefore, brethren, since we have the confidence to enter the Holy Place by a new way of living which He inaugurated for us through the veil, that is His flesh, and since we have a great priest over the house of God, let us draw near with a sincere heart in full assurance of faith, having our hearts sprinkled clean from an evil conscience, and our bodies washed with pure water"* (Hebrews 10:19-22 NASB 1995). What a shame it would have been if we were stuck in the Outer Court forever, which was the case for the regular Israelites, or imagine if we could only make it as far as the Holy Place for the ordinary priest and never go beyond!

PRAYER

Heavenly Father, how I love Your Presence; it is heaven to me. I long to worship You daily. With all I have, and with all that is within me, I live to worship You, Lord. I give You my heart today, I give You my will, and commit to worship You for who You are, in every season of my soul. I pray that You create in me a pure heart and renew a steadfast spirit within me. Search me within, and should You find any idols in my heart, I give You permission to dethrone them. You alone Lord, are worthy to sit on the throne of my heart. As I lift my voice to pray to You and press into Your Presence in worship, may my prayers be counted as incense, with a sweet-smelling aroma and be acceptable before You Holy God. Amen.

SECTION D

THE POWER IN HIS

PRESENCE

THE ENCOUNTER

"And there I will meet with you, and I will speak with you from above the mercy seat" (Exodus 25:22).

"Without intentionally living a holy life daily, we will be like the rest of the regular priests, spending the rest of our lives serving in the Inner and Outer Court and never getting to experience the fullness of God's Presence" (anonymous)

As we embarked on this journey that ushers us into the Presence of God, firstly, we entered through the gate leading us to the Bronze Altar in the Outer Court. There we received the atoning blood of Jesus Christ through faith in Him, our sins were forgiven and we presented our bodies as living sacrifices to God, laying ourselves on the Altar; we also laid our burdens thereon. Next, we progressed to the Bronze Laver, and we looked into the mirror of His Word. As we caught our reflection, we washed with the water of His Word, and we were cleansed and sanctified. We then progressed into the Inner Court, a place of less noise. We fed on Him, the bread of life, at the Table of the Showbread and our inner man was nourished and our emotions were aligned with Him. As we progressed to the Menorah, the oil of His Holy Spirit filled us, and the light of His Word working with His Holy Spirit illuminated us; our minds were lit up. We then proceeded to the Golden Altar, where we communed with Him from deep within our hearts and with a pure heart; the incense of our prayers and our worship ascended before God as a beautiful fragrance, a sweet-smelling aroma acceptable before His Majesty. Thankfully, the veil of separation that stood before the Holy of Holies and hindered us from entering His Presence was torn from top to bottom when our Saviour was crucified. We can now enter in confidently through faith in our Lord Jesus, our Intercessor, our High Priest, and by His precious blood. Through faith in Him alone, we boldly enter into the Holy of Holies, right into the very Presence of God, into a place where we can encounter and know Him intimately and are infused with His Power.

The Ark of the Testimony.

The Ark of the Testimony was the only treasure in the Holy of Holies. The Lord spoke to Moses and gave him instructions on how the Ark of the Testimony was to be built in Exodus 25:10-22.

- It was made of acacia wood.

- It was two and a half cubits long, a cubit and a half wide, and a cubit and a half high.

- It was overlaid with pure gold, inside and out, and had a moulding of gold all around.

- It had four rings of gold in its four corners, two rings on each of the two sides.

- Two poles made of acacia wood and overlaid with gold were also made, put into the Ark's rings for carrying it, and were never to be taken out from it.

The Ark of the Covenant

In addition to this, Moses was instructed to make:

- A mercy seat (a lid for the Ark) of pure gold, two and a half cubits long, a cubit and a half wide.
- Two cherubim of gold, one at either end of the Mercy Seat, and they were one piece with the Mercy Seat.
- The cherubim wings would be stretched out covering the Mercy Seat, the cherubim faced one another, and their faces were facing downward towards the Mercy Seat.

The Mercy Seat would be placed on top of the Ark. The Ark of the Covenant was the throne of God, and it was designed as a throne. God spoke from above the Ark. And inside the Ark were the following three items:

- Two tablets of the Testimony (10 Commandments).
- Aaron's rod that budded (Numbers 17:10).
- A pot of manna (Exodus 16:33).

Once a year, on the Day of Atonement, Aaron the High Priest would go into the Holy of Holies. No one was allowed in the Tabernacle on this day except the High Priest. Firstly, would sacrifice a bull for his sins and his household first, and then with a censer, he would take burning coals from the Altar and a handful of incense into the Holy of Holies, placing the incense before the Mercy Seat as an act of intercession, and a cloud of incense would arise and cover God's Mercy Seat so that the priest would not die (Leviticus 16:12-13). This smoke from burning incense created a veil that protected the High Priest from directly encountering the glory of God as His glory is too powerful to be encountered by a mere human (Exodus 33:20).

Then Aaron would take the blood of the bull and sprinkle the Mercy Seat. Afterwards, he would sacrifice a goat for the sins of the children of Israel and sprinkle the blood on the Mercy Seat and purify it from the people's sins. Finally, Aaron would then atone for the Holy Place and then the Outer Court by anointing the Altar's horns with the blood of the bull and the goat. He would then lay his hands on the head of the scapegoat in the Outer Court as he confessed the people's sins over it and sent it off into the wilderness for good. As the blood of animals was never sufficient to completely wipe away the people's sins, the High Priest and the children of Israel carried out this ritual year in and year out.

What lessons can we draw from the Holy of Holies?
Holiness unto the Lord.

The Holy of Holies was the holiest place in the Tabernacle. The Ark of the Covenant was the only treasure contained in the Holy of Holies. It could not be touched directly by anyone except the High Priest and could only be transported using poles, underscoring its holiness. The poles had to stay in the rings and not be removed so that no one would accidentally touch the gold rings as they inserted the poles. As you would expect, holiness for the High Priest was a prerequisite to enter the Holy of Holies. The word of God tells us that without holiness, we cannot see the Lord (Hebrews 12:14).

God's desire has always been to fellowship with us, which we can trace back to the Garden of Eden when He walked with Adam "in the cool of the day" and the word "walk" in its original Hebrew means to "fellowship". However, because of Adam's sin, which corrupted humanity, we could no longer walk closely to the Lord, for He is too holy. When you look at the multitude of priests who served in the Tabernacle, only one priest could get in the Presence of God. Apart from his clothing which distinguished him from the rest, he also had the words "HOLINESS TO THE LORD" clearly marked on the forehead of his hat or turban, which he wore throughout the year. I believe this emphasised "Holiness unto the Lord" as being at the forefront of his ministry, not just on the Day of Atonement but all year long. This holiness prerequisite rings true for us today, now that we are the priests over God's Temple. *Without intentionally living a holy life daily, we will be like the rest of the regular priests. We will spend the rest of our lives serving in the Inner and Outer Court and never get to experience the fullness of His*

Presence. He who called us is holy and He says, *"Be holy, for I am holy"* (1 Peter 1:16).

Christ is our Mercy Seat, our Propitiation.

The cherubim are known to guard the entrance to God's Presence. They were found on top of the Mercy Seat. They faced downward toward the Mercy Seat rather than facing the entrance to the Holy of Holies. The cherubim are a sign that the way to the Presence of God was downward where they faced, we have to encounter the Mercy Seat first. The High Priest had to smear blood on the Mercy Seat to atone for his sins and the sins of the people. It is only the blood of Jesus that qualifies us today to approach God's Presence and reconciles us to the Father. Christ is our Mercy Seat, our Propitiation (Romans 3:25). Our righteousness is as filthy rags before God (Isaiah 64:6).

A place of Intimacy.

The Holy of Holies was totally dark and, therefore, a place of faith in which the believer, when they walk in cannot see or understand. God Himself becomes our source of light should we choose to trust Him. We enter by faith into a place of an intimate relationship with the Lord. Just like any other relationship, it is built on love, trust, communication, and openness. We get to tell Him all our most minor cares, hurts, and deepest desires without fear of judgement *"Behold, you desire truth in the inward parts"* (Psalm 51:6). We get to lean not on our own understanding but we acknowledge Him, and He then directs our paths (Proverbs 3:5).

The Holy of Holies is a place of total surrender. We surrender everything, our bodies, lives, hearts, plans, and desires. In the Outer Court, at the Bronze Altar, we give our bodies, in the Inner Court at the Golden Altar, we offer our heart, our soul, and in the Holy of Holies, we give our everything. We surrender our whole life to Him. We give ourselves wholly without any barriers, and He moulds us according to His plan for our lives and fills us to enable us to fulfil every God-ordained purpose under heaven.

The Holy of Holies is a place of peace and stillness. It is a place where we have no distractions, and we give Him our undivided attention. We get to minister to the Lord Himself, unlike in the Outer or Inner courts where the priests ministered primarily to the people. God wants us to commune with Him, and He wants an intimate relationship with us, individually. When we get to this place where we are entirely focused on Him, we can hear and discern His voice as we get to know Him more. He speaks to us, and we can hear His voice.

Unlike in the Outer and Inner Court, where the priests served alongside others, entering in the Holy of Holies, which is God's very Presence, is a personal journey, where we get to minister to the Lord on a one-to-one basis and receive from Him. We enter the secret place, a place where we ought to be like Mary rather than Martha. Martha was too consumed with activity for God rather than intimacy with Him (Luke 10:38-42). Martha was so distressed when Jesus visited with them as she was not getting any help from Mary to make the necessary preparations for the Lord, and she took up her complaint to the Lord. The Lord kindly told Martha that Mary had chosen the best part, which no one could take away from her. So, Mary chose to sit at Jesus' feet, to listen attentively to Him and to receive from and of Him.

God ultimately wants us to serve Him as we serve humanity, but first, we must sit at His feet where we are empowered and get clear direction in line with the wonderful plan and purpose He has for our lives. God has a unique purpose for every one of us. But this is revealed to us when we get a revelation of who He is when we spend intimate time with Him. When we develop a meaningful relationship with Him, He can trust us more and He will begin to reveal more of Himself to us and unveil His plans and purpose for our lives progressively, as He leads us by His Holy Spirit.

God wants to be with us, and His Word calls us to draw near to Him *"Draw near to God, and He will draw near to you"*

(James 4:8). He promises to reveal Himself to us when we seek Him with all our hearts, *"And you will seek Me and find Me, when you search for Me with all your heart"* (Jeremiah 29:13). *"The Lord is near to all who call upon Him, to all who call upon Him in truth"* (Psalm 145:18*).* Entering this place is a choice; it is a decision we individually must make. As we draw near to Him with intercession and our worship, as we worship with pure hearts, the incense of our prayers and worship rises before the Mercy Seat, that is a fragrant acceptable before God, a sweet-smelling aroma. He then releases His glory and fills us up.

Revelation and Resurrected Ministry.

Inside the Ark of the covenant was Aaron's rod that budded, which is a picture of resurrection life and ministry. This is your ministry which is in your spirit. When the children of Israel rebelled against Moses and Aaron, God confirmed His choice of servant to minister before Him by way of a rod that resurrected to life, so to speak, and blossomed. Aaron's rod and those of the house of Levi among all the Israelites blossomed, confirming their ministry (Numbers 17). The revelation of this ministry comes forth through intimacy with the Lord. As we surrender totally, God speaks to us. *"And there I will meet with you, and I will speak with you from above the Mercy Seat, from between the two cherubim which are on the Ark of the Testimony, about everything which I will give you in commandment to the children of Israel"* (Exodus 25:22).

In His Presence, our inner man and our gifts of the Spirit are stirred up and cannot help but come to life. We can then identify with the unique individual that God created us to be and function in our divine purpose. *In His Presence, we find authentic freedom.* We cannot help but flourish for as long as we are continually planted and firmly rooted in Him.

On the Mount of the Lord, there is vision.

When God called Abraham to go up to Mount Moriah and sacrifice unto Him the son he loved, Abraham did not hold back the son of promise. Mount Moriah, now known as Mount Zion is a place associated with sacrifice. The plateau of Mount Moriah is where the Jerusalem Temple was eventually built, and where our Lord Jesus Christ was later crucified; at the peak of Mount Moriah, Golgotha. When Abraham mounted Mount Moriah, it was a picture of him ascending into the Temple of God, pressing right into His Presence to sacrifice all he had unto God. As we know, just before he cut his son, an Angel of the Lord appeared immediately, commanding Abraham not to cut his son (Genesis 22:10-12).

Though Abraham did not sacrifice his son, Isaac was sacrificed in Abraham's heart and God's eyes. Abraham had sacrificed his all unto God and his sacrifice was pleasing and acceptable to the Lord. God opened Abraham's eyes immediately to see His provision for a sacrifice, which was a ram caught in the thicket by its horns. I believe this ram would have been long caught but Abraham could not see it until he pressed into God's Presence so to speak and sacrificed his all, suddenly his eyes could see (Genesis 22:13). Abraham named the site *"Adonai Yireh"*. *"Yireh"* comes from the Hebrew verb *"lirot"* *which means* "to see, perceive, look". This same root is used to describe someone who can see things that cannot be seen with an ordinary eye, that is a seer or prophet. In the Presence of the Lord, there is vision, and our eyes are opened to see things through His eyes or see what we would not usually see with our naked eye.

On the Mount of the Lord, there is provision.

In the Ark of the Covenant was a jar of manna. Manna is a symbol of God's provision for you and I and our promised land; it is essentially what God has for us. Throughout their wilderness journey, God was with the children of Israel in a pillar of cloud by day and pillar of fire by night. Daily, God provided for them all their needs and sustained them. Whenever God calls us and whatever He calls us to do, He always provides and sustains us if we are obedient. When God called Abraham to go up to Mount Moriah to sacrifice the son he loved and the son of promise, Abraham did not hold back his son. Young Isaac was surprised that they had the fire and wood only yet not the sacrificial lamb for the burnt offering, so he asked his father about it, Abraham's response was, *"My son, God will provide for himself the lamb for a burnt offering"* (Genesis 22:8). Abraham named this site *"Adonai Yireh"*, which, when the whole term is fully translated, means "the Lord will provide".

As l mentioned before, when God spoke to Moses giving Him instructions on how the Tabernacle was to be constructed, He did not start with the Tabernacle itself but with the Ark of the Testimony. I believe this signifies the importance of the Ark of the Testimony and that it was the ultimate destination for entering the Tabernacle. As we started on this journey, our ultimate goal was to be where the Presence of the Lord is, which is essentially His Power. In the Holy of Holies, we come to a place of intimacy with the Lord, we see the light of His glory, He fills us up, and He gives us instruction, *"And there I will meet with you, and I will speak with you from above the mercy seat…about everything which I will give you in commandment to the children of Israel"* (Exodus 25:22).

Today we have a better covenant with the Lord established on better promises, which is the Blood of Jesus (Luke 22:20). We are now His royal priests serving in His

Temple, *"You also, as living stones, are being built up, a spiritual house, a holy priesthood, to offer up spiritual sacrifices acceptable to God through Jesus Christ"* (1 Peter 2:5). Just like the High Priest in the days of old who served in the wilderness Temple and entered the Holy of Holies on the Day of Atonement, we must serve as the priest of God over the Temples of our own body. Thankfully, we no longer have to wait to enter in once a year on the Day of Atonement. We can enter the Holy of Holies every day, as often as we like bearing our incense of worship and intercession and by faith, covered from our sins with the atoning blood of Jesus Christ.

Entering this place of His Presence is a personal choice, we can choose to avoid entering the Holy of Holies and can continue to do whatever we please without God. I know that there are so many ventures we can take in this life, and jumping onto the bandwagon of worldly opportunities is so much easier, swimming along with the rest of the fish. This may not be God's perfect will for you though. God has a specific and unique assignment for each of us, and we can only find out about His purpose for us through intimacy with Him. His plans for our lives are so much higher than anything we can ever come up with or choose to do (Isiah 55:8-9) I once heard a minister of the Word of God say something very profound: *God is not obliged to bless what He has not called you to do. The Bible says, "Unless the Lord builds a house, they who build it labour in vain"*

(Psalm 127:1). The Tabernacle was designed by God as a blueprint and a roadmap for us to draw near to Him and to be in His Presence. God wants to speak to us and tell us what we ought to pursue. I, therefore, encourage you to do all you can to ensure you enter in to His very Presence. God calls us, but we must be diligent enough to make our call and election sure (2 Peter 1:10).

The Tabernacle was a temporary wilderness Temple, and man is God's ultimate Temple. God wants to fill us with His glory. And when we are filled, we can then go out into the world and fill the earth with the light of His glory. This light will shine through our ministry, which is what God is calling us to do. This ministry could be church ministry, entrepreneurship, working in the corporate world or serving the community at large, in fact it could be in anything you feel called to do. Like in Ezekiel's Millennial Temple vision, when we stand in God's calling, we release rivers of living water and flood the earth. We must first go into the Holy of Holies, be filled with His glory, and then we can go out into the world as we radiate with His light and serve effectively in His Name and for His Glory. In His Presence, we are transformed, and when we abide in Him, we are fruitful (John 15:5).

From the Tabernacle structure and through my learning over the years, *I have realised that it is possible to walk with Jesus and still not see Him nor experience His Power.* It is possible to be saved and spend the rest of your life in the Outer Court proclaiming your salvation or even being unsure about your salvation. The disciples walked with Jesus on the road to Emmaus but did not recognise Him, as their eyes were restrained; only when they sat with Him at the table where He broke bread and gave it to them, did he open their eyes and they recognised Him. They had to go into an intimate space and break bread with Him before He opened their eyes. Eventually, when He vanished from their midst, they asked, *"Did not our hearts burn within us while He talked with us on the road, and while He opened the scriptures?* (Luke 24:32). I therefore implore you, to go into that intimate space with the Lord that you may truly see Him.

Jairus was a ruler of the synagogue, and his daughter was ill and at the point of death. When he saw Jesus, he threw himself at His feet (that in itself is an act of worship), and he begged Jesus to come and heal his dying daughter. As Jesus turned round to follow Jairus to his house, so the crowd followed both Jesus and Jairus. Note that the crowd had been following Jesus for quite a while; I expect they got comfortable and familiar with Him. Yet, Jairus recognised who Jesus was and was able to do for him and so pushed his way to the Master's feet and worshipped Him, and guess what? The Lord then turned around to follow Jairus to his home. Because of his act of worship, Jairus got the King of Kings to follow him to His house (Mark 5:22-24), and the crowd too. This is what worship can do for you; what a revelation!

There was also a woman with the issue of blood. Because of her gender (being a woman), she was inferior in society. She also had the issue of blood; thus, she was impure and that made her doubly inferior. She had been in that condition for 12 years, spent a fortune to be made whole, but her money and surgeons could not help her, instead she got worse. But the day she made up her mind to press into Jesus, to lay hold of the hem of His garment, her story was changed forever. She encountered the Lord, and immediately she was made whole (Mark 5:25-29). Glory be to the Lamb of God!

Dear child of God, do you ever find yourself wondering, "Surely there must be more than this?" Are you dissatisfied with simply going to church every Sunday and singing nice songs? Here is the thing, you too can make a firm decision like the woman with the issue of blood, that you are going to approach the Lord yourself and nothing nor no one shall stand in your way. The invitation is open to whosoever will approach Him. Just like the woman who had the issue of blood, push through the crowds and disciples in your way, whatever this may mean to you. It might mean silencing all other voices calling for your attention, dethroning any idols on the throne of your heart, surrendering your heart, your will, even your pride, and giving your all to the Father.

Refuse to follow Jesus daily without experiencing His Power. Every day we are faced with distractions or reasonable excuses not to spend time with the Lord. It is entirely up to you to remove things in your way and to break protocol at times, like the woman with the issue of blood did, so that you can get to the master's feet and lay hold of His hem. The anointing flows downwards (Psalm 133:2) and at the hem there would be a concentration of the anointing and Power of God. Beloved, position yourself in a place of Power, right on your knees (place of prayer and worship), and reach out to Jesus.

What can stand in our way of intimacy with the Lord?

If we look at the priests serving in the Tabernacle, we see that all of the priests except the High Priest spent all of their lives serving between the Outer Court and Inner Court, and they never made it to the Holy of Holies. They never got to experience the fullness of God's Presence; they would only hear about it from the High Priest. Today as children of God and priests over His Temple, we individually have access to the Holy of Holies; however, it is possible to live just like the regular priests in the days of old and spend all our Christian life between the Outer and Inner Courts, or worse still, like the rest of the Israelites, who could only come as far as the Outer

Court. The invitation to enter into God's Presence is open to all, but entering this place is a choice.

The Bible says that: *"If you are **willing** and **obedient**, you shall eat the good of the land"* (Isaiah 1:19). This "good of the land" includes tangible and spiritual blessings and flourishing in every area of our lives. I would also like to think that there are two components to being willing, firstly it is a heart attitude when your heart and mind are made up and set, and the second aspect of this willingness requires action because faith without works is dead (James 2:26).

Concerning obedience, the ten commandments inside the Ark of Covenant were the terms by which God would dwell amid His people and bless them. The same is true for us today; God can only be in our midst if we are obedient to His Word (John 14:23). God's finger wrote the ten commandments on the tablets in the days of old (Exodus 31:18). Today this law is imprinted on our hearts; as we allow the Spirit of God to flow into our hearts, our heart of stone is turned into flesh, and His Word becomes alive within us.

We, therefore, need to do all we need to enter His Presence and refrain from anything that may hinder us from entering in. Various reasons may stand in our way:

◉ **Laziness** – Where we don't enter His Presence just because the price to be paid for pressing into God's Presence is too high. The cost could be in the form of our time as we seek His face in prayer, worship, or studying His Word. This cost could also be financial as we give Him our financial sacrifices and offerings. In terms of relationships; this may mean spending less time with our loved ones or even in some cases letting go of unhealthy relationships, and sometimes means giving up some of your sleep as and when His Spirit leads us.

◉ **Fear** – Perhaps fear is caused by wrong beliefs, past encounters, or even a fear of letting go of control of our lives and allowing God to be the Lord of our lives.

◉ **Busy lifestyle** – We could perhaps be too busy serving the Lord like Martha was and so neglect sitting at His feet like Mary did. We could also be busily preoccupied with our personal motives or busy running our own errands.

◉ **Blessings** – Our blessings can also be a hindrance from worshipping and serving the Lord. We can find ourselves too busy enjoying our blessings such as spouses, children, jobs, wealth, etc. As a result, we cannot make or set aside meaningful time with the Lord.

- **Distractions** – In this day and age, we can easily be distracted by social media and media such as TV. We could also be distracted by people around us.

- **Sin** – which results in guilt or hardness of heart. Sin could be sexual immorality such as fornication and adultery, it could also be gossiping; the list goes on and on. When sin enters our hearts and we are living a sinful life, our natural response would be to run away from God like Adam and Eve did in the Garden of Eden. When we cannot see God in our unrepentant state; we cannot enter the Holy of Holies.

- **Seared Consience** – Due to the cares of the world, our heart is divided between God and things of the world. Being surrounded by a wrong and corrupt company can make us so accommodating and indifferent to sin, such that we tolerate ungodly practices, behaviours, and conversations. Discerning God's voice and the move of His Spirit in such conditions becomes difficult. Our hearts become hardened and we become insensitive to the Holy Spirit.

- **Offences** – Choosing to be offended by people close to us, such as family, friends, work colleagues, and people we trust and look up to could also prevent us from entering His Presence. Offence caused by brethren too can be so damaging, I have seen many stumbling because of that. Be quick to forgive as God has forgiven, releasing the burden of any bitterness or hardness towards that person.

- ⊙ **Shame** – Due to abuse, failure in the past, or poor self-esteem and feeling of unworthiness.

- ⊙ **Doubt** – perhaps you have tried in the past and given up too soon because of doubt, Or maybe due to wrong seeds sown into your mind by the enemy.

Jesus spoke about the parable of a sower who went out to sow, *"But other seed fell on good ground and yielded a crop that sprang up, increased and produced: some thirtyfold, some sixty and some a hundred"* (Mark 4:8). In our walk with the Lord, a thirtyfold harvest is equivalent to an Outer Court relationship, a sixtyfold harvest represents an Inner Court relationship, and the hundredfold harvest signifies a relationship characterised by fullness of the Presence of God, which is experienced beyond the veil, in the Holy of Holies. It is only in the fullness of His Presence that we can receive the fullness of all He has for us. Thus, we receive every blessing, His Presence, peace, and His Power which is His anointing. And our very lives will be characterised with so much fruitfulness. I do not know about you, beloved, but l would rather have all that the Lord has for me. So, let us press on and in.

Apostle Paul wrote, "*but I press on, that I may lay hold of that for which Christ Jesus has also laid hold of me, … I press toward the goal for the prize of the upward call of God in Christ Jesus*" (Philippians 3:12, 14).

Developing and cultivating a relationship with the Lord.

Having an encounter with the Presence of the Lord is such an exciting thing, but this should not be a one-off thing. Like any other relationship, you need to cultivate and maintain the intimacy of this relationship and guard it diligently for you to produce fruit continually. Jesus said, "*I am the vine, you are the branches. He who abides in Me, and I in him, bears much fruit; for without Me you can do nothing*" (John 15:5). If we do not remain in Him, we will wither spiritually, and cannot bear fruit.

Below are some of the tips for developing and maintaining this relationship:

- Invite Him into your day, have casual conversations even during your chores.
- Set aside time with Him and spend quality time with Him.
- Have regular communication and have a meeting place.
- Protect your time with the Lord by cutting out external interruptions; however, always allowing the Holy Spirit to interrupt you.

⊙ Make time for stillness and to listen. Prayer is a two-way street; ultimately, we want to hear Him speak to us, and tell us what to do.

⊙ Enter into the Outer Court, but do not pitch your permanent tent there. Instead, press into the Holy of Holies, never get comfortable, and never cease to be in awe of His Presence.

⊙ Seek Him when you have a need, but most importantly, seek Him for no reason, just because you can and you want to be with Him.

⊙ Remember, *you are unique; do not be imitators of men. God wants to have a custom-made relationship with you.*

The Bible says that *"the people who know their God shall be strong and carry out great exploits"* (Daniel 11:32). The secret of being fruitful is in knowing God for yourself first, and not just knowing about God. Beloved, I pray that you will have the willpower to press into the Holy of Holies, into the very Presence of God, so to speak, and like apostle Paul prayed, that this will be your prayer too: ***"That I may know Him and the Power of His resurrection,*** (Philippians 3:10), the same power that raised our Lord Jesus Christ from the dead (Ephesians 1:19-21 CEV).

Prayer

Lord, You said in Your Word that If I seek You, I will find You when I search for You with all my heart. I desire to know You intimately, and I give my heart to You, Lord. I let go of all my guards, and I surrender my all to You, I give You my heart, my soul, my life, my dreams, my deepest and most secret desires, be the Lord of it all. Thank you today that I can access Your very Presence; the veil of separation was torn, and today I can boldly enter the Holy of Holies by the blood of Jesus.

As I seek You, reveal yourself to me. Give me vision, give me revelation, give me wisdom, reveal Your wonderful plan and purpose for my life. Show me Your glory and fill me till I overflow. Cause me to radiate so brightly with the light of Your glory, as I give back to You in service in whatever form You are calling me to serve You as I seek to bring great glory and honour to Your name. Amen.

GOD-CONFIDENCE

"On the other side of fear lies freedom" (anonymous)

"For God has not given us a spirit of fear, but of
Power and of love and of a sound mind"
(2 Timothy 1:7)

Now that you have encountered Him and received His anointing, His Dunamis power, to do what God calls you to do, you need to understand that this Power is just potential energy, just like dynamite. Without ignition, nothing will change. "It is action that separates achievers from dreamers" (anonymous). In my walk with the Lord, 1 have come to understand that it is quite possible to be full of the anointing of God yet bear no fruit. It is possible to achieve nothing on this earth and take your anointing with you to your grave. Quite often, we are crippled by fear and unbelief. Les Brown wrote that *"The graveyard is the richest place on earth"*, this is a very profound statement.

I am reminded of the parable of talents: a master who was travelling to a far country entrusted his three servants with talents; five to one, two to the other, and one to the last one according to their abilities. On His return, he called his servants to give an account. The first two servants had doubled their talents and received the master's praise, and the third servant who had received one talent safeguarded his talent instead and did not increase it. As a result, he received condemnation from his master and was judged "wicked and lazy" (Matthew 25:14-26). This parable applies to us too; when The Lord entrusts us with all kinds of gifts, we are essentially stewards, and he wants us to be both fruitful and faithful. But when we safeguard because of fear or unbelief, we are like the third servant condemned and judged as wicked and lazy. There are, of course, times when God opens doors for us supernaturally, but in most cases, we must rise above fear, and take action.

But what is Confidence?

Confidence (noun) is defined in www.dictionary.com as below (noun):

1. complete trust; belief in the powers, trustworthiness, or reliability of a person or thing.
2. belief in oneself and one's powers or abilities; self-confidence; self-reliance; assurance.
3. certitude; assurance.

True confidence comes from within us and not external things such as materials, our social circle, or achievements.

Confidence is a feeling and is stemmed from our thoughts. Our confidence level is not static but tends to fluctuate. I call to mind a great prophet of God, Elijah. God used him mightily to showcase His Power and destroy the 400 prophets of Baal. So, it is pretty evident the anointing of God was in him, and he was so confident in the Power of God. But shortly after this victory, **fear** crept into his mind, and he believed the lie of the enemy, his confidence diminished, and he ran away from Jezebel into the cave. His confession even changed; he wanted to die! (1 Kings 19:4.)

Benefits of Confidence.

Being a confident person comes with many benefits, such as being open to trying new things outside of your comfort zone, an open attitude to learning from others, and taking on challenges as God leads you, trusting that He is with you. You are more likely to be able to resist the temptation to constantly compare yourself to others but embrace your God-given uniqueness and use it to your advantage as a competitive edge.

Healthy confidence levels usually come along with freedom and authenticity. You will also have faith in your God-given abilities trusting that God is with you, He is ordering your steps, and that His grace is all-sufficient to do what He is calling you to do. When you are a confident person, you can build healthy boundaries, decide for yourself and say "no" when you need to say it, and not feel the need to go with the flow which helps in having a better relationship with the Lord.

You will also have clarity of mind and the ability to hear and discern God's voice and will for your life, and you would most likely make healthy and quality decisions without the need to impress other people. You are likely to have a positive attitude and mindset and be resilient. As for us children of God, our confidence is not our own, but it is the confidence that is rooted in the one inside us. It is essentially **God-Confidence**. The opposite of this confidence is **fear,** which comes about when we believe the enemy's lies more than what we believe God says about us.

So, where does fear come from?

Fear is rooted in our beliefs, and we generally learn our beliefs from people around us and the environments we live in, mainly at a young age. Every child is born with a natural state of being confident. *"But You are He who took me out of the womb; You made me trust while on my mother's breasts"* (Psalm 22:9). As we grow older, we are naturally conditioned to think in a specific way. From the environments and societies we grow up in, we learn and adopt beliefs. We even adopt beliefs of people we look up to, spend time with, and listen to often enough, and we begin to believe their version of the truth as our own. Bad experiences in life can also instil beliefs that cause fear in us and knock our confidence, bad experiences such as depression, loss, disappointment, unemployment, divorce, grief, ill health, rejection, etc. They all affect different individuals differently.

Your beliefs will shape how you live your life, and your brain will always regulate you out to the current belief you have. When you are so locked into your beliefs, you live a limited life that you will not see anything good beyond the boundaries of your beliefs. You even decide things beforehand and refuse to see a different picture or accept another version of the truth. You will look for evidence to affirm your beliefs, and you become very selective and filter what you let in and what you keep out.

Your beliefs determine your destiny. However, the good thing is that your beliefs are not static; you can always change them. It is a personal choice as you are always in control of your thoughts and beliefs, *the power is in your hands*. Whether you are responsible or not for the unhelpful beliefs you hold that cause a knock on your confidence, you can choose to take full accountability for them from now on.

Here are biblical comparisons of two great men of Israel who responded differently to an opportunity to glorify God. One lived in fear, and the other was a confident warrior.

A. Gideon (Judges 6 and 7)

In the Lord's eyes, Gideon was a leader, a judge over the Israelites, and a mighty man. God called Gideon, and yet he lived such a defeated life. Though he lived in the mountains, he shamefully lived in caves, hiding from the Midianites. Along with the Israelites, Gideon lived a greatly impoverished life. Every season the Midianites would come up to destroy their harvest, year after year. The Lord appeared to him and called him "a mighty man of valour" (Judges 6:12). The Lord then spoke to Gideon and commissioned him to rise and wage war against the Midianites to save the Israelites from their oppression.

He commanded him to go and assured him of victory as the Lord Himself had sent him. The Lord said, *"Go in this might of yours and you shall save Israel from the hand of the Midianites. Have I not sent you?"* Judges (6:14). Because of his fear, he responded poorly to the Lord, the one who had created him and made him judge over the Israelites and even called him a "mighty man", by reciting all the negative things about himself. He told the Lord that "his clan was the weakest in Manasseh and that he was the least in his father's house".

In spite of his negative confessions, the Lord assured Gideon that He will be with him and that he will prevail against the Midianites. Gideon began to doubt if it was God speaking to him and asked God for a sign (Judges 6:17), and after the Lord consumed the meat and the leavened bread placed on the rock for which Gideon had requested for a sign, Gideon believed it was the Lord speaking to Him.

The Lord then asked Gideon to destroy the altar of Baal, which his father had built, and to build an Altar to the Lord. Gideon believed the Lord spoke to him after the miraculous sign, yet he was still afraid of men. Gideon chose to do as the Lord had commanded him in the night rather than in the day, in the sight of all men to see. *"So Gideon took ten men from among his servants and did as the Lord had said to him. But because he feared his father's household and the men of the city too much to do it by day, he did it by night"* (Judges 6:27).

Gideon later asks God to confirm again that He will deliver Israel by his hand, which the Lord had already assured him. Gideon then asked for two signs of the fleece: a dewy fleece on dry ground and a dry fleece on the dewy ground, and the Lord performed the two signs. And finally, Gideon went to war with 300 Israelites and prevailed over the Midianites.

B. David (1 Samuel 17)

Scripture records David as "a man after God's own heart". Though the youngest of eight sons, a lowly shepherd looked down on by his warrior brothers, undervalued and almost insignificant in his father's eyes, David was a self-confident man. David had every reason to have no confidence at all but chose and made up his mind to trust in the Power of His God, the Lord of Hosts. When Goliath challenged the armies of Israelites day in and day out, David the confident warrior, witnessed this the day he came to the scene and posed this question *"For who is this uncircumcised Philistine, that he should defy the armies of the living God?"* (1 Samuel 17:26). David was not yet a king, though he was anointed king already. David knew that God was with him and remembered that he had fought and killed both a bear and a lion in the past as he defended his father's sheep, so he saw an opportunity to serve and glorify God, and he went hard after it with such confidence. His confidence was rooted in his God. He went face to face with Goliath, the giant on the battlefield, and killed him in the sight of all men, unlike Gideon!

Goliath was a man so mighty in stature, and for forty days, morning and evening, he presented himself before the Israel army and defied them. Still, they were all too afraid of this Philistines "champion". But when the bold David came to the scene and witnessed all that, he challenged the status quo. King Saul was even doubtful as David was too youthful, but David would not relent. Eventually, Saul gave David his armour. However, on trying them on, David, a man who confidently trusted in the Lord's Power, declined the king's armour, and I love what he said: "*I cannot walk with these for I have not tested them*" (1 Samuel 17:39). David had tested and seen the Power of God working in his life and had no reason to believe that this time around the Lord will fail him. He was happy to go into battle, trusting in the Lord's Power and nothing else.

On the battlefield, Goliath spoke to David and defied him as he had always done to the Israeli armies. This war started with words, and what I love about David's attitude is that he did not keep quiet; he engaged immediately in this war of words. He spoke back and declared the Power of his God to the enemy "*But I come to you in the Name of the Lord of hosts, the God of the armies of Israel whom you have defied. This day the Lord will deliver you into my hand, and I will strike you and take your head from you and this day I will give the carcasses of the camp of the Philistines to the birds of the air and the wild beasts of the earth, that all the earth may know that there is a God in Israel*" (1 Samuel 17:45-46). When Goliath arose and drew near to meet David, David did not flee like his brothers and the armies of the Israelites. In the sight of all men (unlike Gideon), David hurried and ran toward the enemy to meet and slay him. What a showcase of confidence! Just like David had declared, the Lord God indeed delivered Goliath into David's hand, and he prevailed over him. Glory be to God!

Sadly, Gideon's story is a reality for many Christians today. Though a mighty man called by God, Gideon lacked confidence in God and himself and preferred to live in hiding from his purpose. He was afraid of man. Though anointed by God, Gideon chose to live a defeated life, in the cave, over a life where he would challenge the status quo. When the Lord called him "mighty man," he responded with words that highlighted his weakness, how he saw himself and unbelief in who God said he was. So, when the Lord commissioned him to go and fight the enemy, he needed more than one sign for assurance.

God has called every one of His children to glorify Him and bring honour to His Name. But the majority are sadly paralysed and held hostage by fear: fear of man and the unknown, lack of confidence in God and themselves, complacency, and many other factors. But as for the courageous David, The Lord used him mightily, unlike Gideon.

What lessons can we draw from the two:

- ⦿ Believe in God. Do not fear man.
- ⦿ When the enemy speaks to you, talk back.
- ⦿ When the enemy advances toward you, invoke the name of the Lord of Hosts and go to meet him immediately in boldness.

- You can still be anointed, called by God, yet live a defeated life.

- When you seek God's heart, fear cannot have a hold over you.

- The more confidence you have in God, the more He is likely to use you mightily.

How can you overcome fear?

Identify the stronghold first.

First, you must identify this stronghold of fear and its origin and then refrain from telling past or negative stories repeatedly. It does not change the outcome, but the negative feelings grow stronger. For such a long time, I have had such fear of public speaking. I even attended a public speaking course, but when I finished, I was even more afraid and nervous to speak in public because I still believed that I was not good at it. I lacked confidence because of one bad experience. Back in 2013, I confidently volunteered to speak in front of an audience of about 50 people. I had no written script and sadly, I forgot what I wanted to say in the middle of the speech. Trying to remember in front of over 50 pairs of eyes staring you in the face was too intense, unbearable, and made things worse. I went completely quiet and must have taken nearly another 60 seconds or so to finally get my thoughts back on track and open my mouth again. That was the longest 60 seconds of my life; it felt like a whole year. I had never felt so ashamed and daft for as long as I could remember. After that, I convinced myself how useless I was at public speaking, and I made a covenant with myself to never do it again and to never make a fool of myself again.

I would retell the story of how awful I was, and in so doing I strengthened my negative belief in the retelling. The truth is I had one experience and projected that one event into all future events. But my truth still stood until I learned to change my beliefs and align with the word of God. A story was once told: "*A Native American grandfather talked to his grandson about how he felt. He said, 'I feel as if I have two wolves fighting in my heart. One wolf is the vengeful, angry, and violent one. The other wolf is the loving, compassionate one.' The grandson asked him, 'Which wolf will win the fight in your heart?' The grandfather answered: 'The one I feed.'*" This is why we need to know what the Word of God says about us and feed our soul with this Word and confess over and over again until we believe it because the wolf that you feed is the one that wins, and in this case, it is the beliefs that you meditate on. Only the truth of God's Word can set you free, therefore find out His truth.

Use our weapons to overcome fear.

"For the weapons of our warfare are not carnal, but mighty in God for pulling down strongholds, casting down arguments and every high thing that exalts itself against the knowledge of God, bringing every thought into captivity to the obedience of Christ" (2 Corinthians 10:4-5). Strongholds operate in our minds and will keep us captive unless we face them and tear them down. Our biggest battlefield is the mind. The mind is so powerful, and the Bible says, *"For as he thinks in his heart, so is he"* (Proverbs 23:7). The weapon we have to pull down strongholds is the Word of God. Strongholds are beliefs we hold that are contrary to the word of God. Our thoughts, which can also be our idols, will eventually become our beliefs and, consequently, our strongholds if meditated on long enough. Idols are things that are exalted in our hearts and hinder us from giving God priority. Thankfully, we do not have to trust in our thoughts and beliefs, but our confidence is in Him who is inside us and His unshakeable Word.

Because of their unbelief and hardness of heart, the Israelites could not enter into the promised land. God brings us out so that He can lead us in. God delivers us for a purpose, "so that…" But quite often, we get excited about the "deliverance" and are not interested in "Purpose". The Israelites had the faith to leave Egypt but not to enter Canaan, the land of promise. The above is the very same picture we paint when we accept Jesus Christ as our Lord and Saviour, we are justified and never leave the Outer Court to explore or press in to discover and fulfil what God has in store for us in the Holy of Holies.

We are not willing to pay the price to have an intimate deeper relationship with the Lord, allowing us to walk in His Power. He says in His Word that He created you and I for a specific assignment, to bring glory and honour to His Name. Think about this! But this takes the courage of Joshua and Caleb (Numbers 13). We have to choose to see ourselves through the eyes of our God and have the courage and determination like Caleb to arise immediately and go and possess the land. Caleb boldly declared "for we are well able to overcome it" (Numbers 13:30). It might be a fearful thing to do, but that's okay; you can still trust in the one who called you and go ahead. "Feel the fear and do it anyway" (Susan Jeffers). Confidence is never the absence of fear, and our confidence is not in our abilities, but it is rooted in the all-powerful and faithful God who lives inside us. Will you choose faith over fear today? Will you choose obedience over disobedience?

Practical steps to cultivate Self-Confidence.

1. **Self-Audit:**

   - ⊙ When you say I do not have the confidence, what precisely do you mean?

   - ⊙ In what areas of your life do you lack confidence?

   - ⊙ Identify where your perceived lack of confidence has come from.

2. **Unlearn** – You unlearn by finding out the truth first, which is found in God's Word and promises. It is the truth of God's Word that will set you free (John 8:32). Renounce every false belief you have ever believed and break covenant with it. When you now know the truth, the next step is to start creating new beliefs.

3. **Affirm** – Based on the truth of God's Word, write down your positive affirmations, e.g., ten scriptures, then personalise them to make "I AM" or "I CAN" Statements. Confess these affirmations daily or as often as possible. Such as confessing that *"I can do all things through Christ which strengthens me"* (Philippians 4:13) and *"I am bold as a lion"* (Proverbs 28:1b). Confess with faith, nothing wavering, and be fully persuaded of these truths. The more you confess and hear these

words, the more this will create different thought patterns in you, which will, in turn, create a new self-image and then produce new positive behaviours. "*So then faith comes by hearing, and hearing by the word of God* " (Romans 10:17).

4. **Act on your beliefs** – It is excellent to have a vision, but faith without works is dead. Draw a road map to accomplish your vision, if you have not done one already, outlining the steps you need to take to get there and the steps you need to begin to take, trusting that He who is inside you is so much greater than the one in the world and that your confidence has a great reward. I call to mind the story of Caleb and Joshua, the courageous Israeli spies who, along with the other ten spies, were sent out by Moses at the Lord's command to spy out the promised land of Canaan. After surveying the land of promise, the other ten spies returned with a bad report. They confessed that the land's inhabitants were strong, even more potent than themselves; the cities were fortified and large. Interestingly, in their confession, they never mentioned the name of the Lord; they further confessed they had seen the giants (descendants of Anak), and that they (the ten spies), were like grasshoppers in their own

eyes, they even projected their self-image to that of the giants view of them; *"we were like grasshoppers in our own sight, and so we were in their sight"* (Numbers 13:33). Though they had seen the good of the land and all its fruit, not only did they refuse to go face the giants and possess the land, but they also instilled fear in the whole camp of the Israelites.

Caleb and Joshua, in contrast, rose up in faith with such great positivity. They gave a good report of the land, mentioned the name of the Lord, and encouraged the people not to rebel against Him. They urged the Israelites not to be afraid of the inhabitants as the Lord's hand was against them, but His protection was upon the Israelites. Though the twelve spies had seen the same land, their fortified cities, and the giants in there, Caleb and Joshua chose to see them through a lens of faith, through the eyes of our great God. The evil report of the ten spies and resulting fear of the people aroused the anger of the Lord against all His people, and He vowed that their generation would never see the promised land save Caleb and Joshua, who brought a good report and believed in their God.

Let me bring you to the remembrance of the story of the four lepers (2 Kings 7:3-20) who stayed at the entrance to the city gate in Samaria during a famine. Because of their leprosy, they were considered unclean and, therefore, outcasts in society. The lepers one day decided to go into the camp of the enemy, the Syrians at twilight. And at the very same time, twilight, the Bible also records that God caused their enemies to hear footsteps that were amplified, and they ran, leaving behind all their possessions. As the lepers advanced into the enemy's camp, they found the camp deserted, and the lepers laid hold of all the enemy's possessions.

What does that mean? We meet God in movement. His Word says, *"Your ears shall hear a word behind you saying, 'This is the way, walk in it, whenever you turn to the right hand or whenever you turn to the left'"* (Isaiah 30:21). When we take practical steps of faith trusting in Him, He despatches warrior angels to fight on our behalf. He sends forth helpers where we need help, and He releases His grace immediately. His grace is all that we need, after all. Though the lepers were physically poor and had to beg for their survival, they were so rich in faith. We might have severe weakness, be marginalised and despised in society just like the lepers were, but

God's Word says, *"My grace is sufficient for you, for My strength is made perfect in weaknesses"* (2 Corinthians 12:9).

5. **Regulate** – It is vital to regulate your new beliefs and ensure you will not drift to the old ones. Here are some suggestions on how to do that:

   ⦿ Continually confess the Word of God over your life and mind.

Pay attention to your internal voices and silence the critical inner voice or talk back to the enemy, but quite often the critical inner voice comes from yourself. Master your self-talk and learn to speak well of yourself always. Practice self-love and celebrate your successes, even if they are small.

   ⦿ Celebrate yourself and exercise gratitude.

In addition, take care of your physical and emotional needs first because you cannot pour from an empty cup. Set healthy boundaries, let go of toxic relationships and remain true to who you are. Learn to see yourself in light of God's Word and love who you are now. Remember that confidence building is a progressive process; it will not happen overnight, so keep at it until you become confident.

Remember:

1. Confidence is not being the loudest person in the room.

2. Confidence is like a muscle; it gets stronger with exercise.

3. Believe in God, focus on where you want to go and not your fears.

4. Prepare and practice.

5. Confidence is not the absence of fear; you can still do it afraid. The Bible is believed to contain 365 "fear-nots", there is therefore enough provision of courage for each day.

Our confidence should not be in what we have or in worldly wisdom. Though all these may help to a certain extent, our confidence has ultimately to be in the One who has called us, God Himself. And we do not direct our energies or focus on what we do not want to see, but we focus more on what we want to see in our lives which is why the Bible tells us to meditate on the Word of God. Then, when we behold our eyes on Jesus, we are transformed into the image of His Glory, and we begin to see more of Him manifesting in our lives.

In my walk with the Lord, I have gone through different seasons of learning. The first thing I learned was worship, such a beautiful thing to sit at the feet of Jesus, forget everything else and worship Him in the beauty of holiness. The next season was learning spiritual warfare. I felt I could take the devil by the horns. But sadly, during that season, I drifted from worshipping and forgot about it and started warfare daily, as many times a day as I could. It got so bad that I woke up one day feeling physically drained and discouraged, so I said to the Lord, "Lord I am so tired of fighting, I do not believe this is the life you called me for, when is this war going to end?"

I heard the Lord speak straight back to me saying, "I never asked you to fight the devil every day. The reason you are fighting the devil daily is that you have exalted him above My name, you have believed the lie of the enemy that he is more powerful than Myself. And whenever you are fighting him, it is because you can't stop thinking about him; you have forgotten your first love. You have forgotten about My power and are operating from a place of fear. It is fear of the enemy and not confidence in My name and My Power!" Ouch. I went down on my knees and cried out to the Lord in repentance. Here is the thing, "You get more of what you focus on". *I focused on the devil and got more of him: fear, anxiety, tiredness, restlessness, and a hardened heart.*

There are times for spiritual warfare prayers, but God wants us to have a healthy balance in prayer and He wants us to keep Him in His place in our lives, right on the throne of our hearts. When you are always up to fight the devil, it is because you are afraid of him, and your focus is on him rather than God; you are more confident of the power of the devil than that of God. When you give the enemy so much attention, he will give you direction. When you are afraid, try worshipping instead!

On the other side of fear lies freedom, *"For God has not given us a spirit of fear, but of Power and of love and of a sound mind"* (2 Timothy 1:7).

Prayer

Lord I thank You that You have not given me a spirit of fear but of power and a sound mind. I repent today for every area of my life where I have believed the enemy's lies and allowed fear to rule in my life. I reaffirm my trust in You, and today I choose to make a firm decision to break, in Your name and power, the shackles of fear that have held me hostage, from moving forth into my divine assignment. I cast down every imagination and every high thing that exalts itself and is contrary to Your Word and counsel for my life, and I bring into captivity every thought to the obedience of Christ. I declare that You are the Lord of my mind, and I have the mind of Christ. Stir up my inner man today and let faith arise in my heart once again. Grant it to me today to rise with boldness like David the mighty warrior and that I will confront and speak to every giant, every uncircumcised Philistine standing in my path and slay it, trusting in the power of my God, Jehovah, the mighty warrior in battle. Amen.

GO FORTH

Now that you have travelled this journey and made it into the Holy of Holies, the very Presence of God, and encountered the Power of His Presence through intimate fellowship with Him, Congratulations! You have put on God-confidence too, now what do you do, and where do you go from here? You need to ask yourself the questions below:

- What are you being called to do?
- Where are you currently?
- Identify the gap and what you need to do to close the gap. For example, do you need some training, learn a new skill, invest in mentorship or coaching?
- Is there something you need to let go of or to do less of (e.g., unhelpful habits, relationships, unhelpful thoughts, non-value creating activities such as spending unnecessary time on social media)?

As you seek to answer the questions above, I recommend the following:

- Pray for clarity and that the Lord will make His way plain before your face (Psalm 5:8).
- Pray for divine direction and counsel.

Remember to consistently pray the Father's will. I cannot promise you that you will like the answer to this prayer nor the process, but I can guarantee you that the end will be glorious. A few years ago, I prayed the Father's will over a situation that the Lord had brought to my attention through an open vision and secondly in a dream.

As a young believer, I did not know how to handle the situation so I prayed to the Lord that His will be done in my life, and immediately after this prayer, I lost my job. I was so livid! After composing myself, I humbly went back to the Lord on my knees and in tears. The Lord assured me that He was in control and He gave me peace. Two weeks after leaving my job without knowing where the next job was, I was offered a new job by another company. It was so beautiful that I didn't even have to attend a formal interview. This company saw my CV, they liked it and invited me to spend half the day with them as I tested the waters, then they offered me the job at the end of the day. That role gave me the career breakthrough I had long prayed for, and consequently changed the trajectory of my career.

Chiefly, remember this: as the priest of God, you are called to minister to Him first and then to His people. Before the Apostles were sent forth to minister to the people, their primary duty was to spend time with Jesus (Mark 3:14).

Therefore, before you go about doing your doings, you need to spend time first with the Lord, and you will be filled and empowered to take every mountain.

I believe the reason you read this book and got this far, is that the Spirit of the Lord is calling you to step out and step up and do exploits in His Name and for His glory. But bear in mind that there are some giants on assignment to intimidate and hinder the children of God. There are giants on assignment to instil fear in you and to stop you in your tracks. That is why you need His power, and this power comes from being in His Presence and through getting acquainted with Him. And Jesus is the only way to the Father's Presence.

You need His Presence to go with you to be able to fight and withstand every giant. Moses understood this very well after spending years with the Lord in the wilderness and seeing what the Presence of God was able to do for him and the children of Israel in Exodus 33. The Lord put him to the test just before departing Mount Sinai for the promised land and asked that they enter in without Him, but Moses blatantly refused and said, "If you will not go with us, if your Presence doesn't come with us, Lord, there is no way we are going to move from here. He had seen and understood that there was deliverance, provision, joy, peace, strength for the journey, and victory for the battle in His Presence. So, beloved, may this be your prayer too as you go forth, "Let your Presence, Oh Lord go before me, be with me, be in me and all around me".

Secondly, in the Temple of God was where the Presence of God dwelt. For as long as the Temple was not defiled or desecrated, God's Presence was right in the Holy of Holies. His Presence signifies His **"Power"**. So, you and I are essentially powerhouses. More so, considering that you and I are now the living Temples of God today. If I bring you to the remembrance of all the material used in the Tabernacle's construction, I come to conclude that you and I are so valuable and worthy!

FINAL DECLARATIONS

Beloved, I therefore encourage you to put on God-confidence, rise up and go forth. So then as you are lifted souls will be drawn unto you, not for your glory, but so that you can show them the way to the Great Master; it is all for His Glory.

Heaven is backing you up, and I declare this to you that you are unstoppable;

I declare this to you that you are bold and fearless;

I declare this to you that you are a Temple of God, beautiful, unique, worthy, a container of the treasure of His Holy Spirit;

You are a powerhouse indeed, full of the Power of God.

May this be your confident and unshakeable confession that "**I am a Temple of God**," worthy and powerful!

Shalom.

"*And let them make me a sanctuary; that I may dwell among them*" *(Exodus 25:8 KJV)*

Printed in Great Britain
by Amazon